To my life-time loyal friend.
Krystal
2020

The Power to Make a Difference

The Power to Make a Difference

Compiled by Beebe Kauffman and Katy Kauffman

Lighthouse Bible Studies

Copyright © 2019 by Lighthouse Bible Studies, LLC

Published by Lighthouse Bible Studies, LLC, PO Box 304, Buford, Georgia 30515

ISBN-13: 978-0-9994857-0-5

All rights reserved. No part of this publication may be reproduced, stored in a retrieval system, or transmitted in any form by any means without the prior written permission of the publisher, except for brief quotations of forty words or less.

Scripture references marked CSB are taken from The Christian Standard Bible. Copyright © 2017 by Holman Bible Publishers. Used by permission. Christian Standard Bible®, and CSB® are federally registered trademarks of Holman Bible Publishers, all rights reserved.

Scripture references marked ESV are taken from The Holy Bible, English Standard Version. ESV® Permanent Text Edition® (2016). Copyright © 2001 by Crossway Bibles, a publishing ministry of Good News Publishers.

Scripture references marked HCSB are taken from Holman Christian Standard Bible (HCSB) Copyright © 1999, 2000, 2002, 2003, 2009 by Holman Bible Publishers, Nashville Tennessee. All rights reserved.

Scripture references marked KJV are taken from the Holy Bible, King James Version.

Scripture references marked NASB are taken from the New American Standard Bible. Copyright © 1960, 1962, 1963, 1968, 1971, 1972, 1973, 1975, 1977, 1995 by The Lockman Foundation.

Scripture references marked NIV are taken from the Holy Bible, New International Version®, NIV® Copyright ©1973, 1978, 1984, 2011 by Biblica, Inc.® Used by permission. All rights reserved worldwide.

Scripture references marked NKJV are taken from the New Kings James Version. Copyright © 1979, 1980,1982 by Thomas Nelson, Inc. Used by permission. All rights reserved.

Scripture references marked NLT are taken from the Holy Bible, New Living Translation copyright© 1996, 2004, 2007 by Tyndale House Publishers Inc.

Scripture references marked TLB are taken from The Living Bible copyright © 1971 by Tyndale House Foundation. Used by permission of Tyndale House Publishers Inc., Carol Stream, Illinois 60188. All rights reserved.

The Message. Copyright © 1993, 2002, 2018 by Eugene H. Peterson.

Interior photos on all pages are public domain photos from pixabay.com.

The Power of Words

Introduction 9

Treasured Words 10
by Jeannie Waters

Speak Life 15
by Krystal Weeks

Weaponizing the Dictionary 19
by Ron Gallagher

Finding Strength in the Words of Life 24
by Connie Wohlford

Silence Negative Self-Talk: Go Beyond the Inner Critic 29
by K. A. Wypych

Wonderful Words of Life 33
by Karen O. Allen

The Power of Encouraging Words 38
by Katherine Pasour

Are Your Words Fitly Spoken? 44
by Dorcas Asercion Zuniga

Hitting Pause on Words That Wound 49
by Lori Brown

Of Butter and War, Oil and Swords 53
by Mary Albers Felkins

The Power of Doing

Introduction 57

Overwhelmed Is a Good Place to Be 58
by Marilyn Nutter

Serving God in a Season of Brokenness 62
by Lori Brown

Weakness: The Devastating Impact of Doing Nothing 67
by Ron Gallagher

Share the Love 71
by Katherine Pasour

The Power of Consistency 76
by Barbara Latta

Be Anxious for Nothing 80
by Dorcas Asercion Zuniga

Let Go of Dangerous Things 84
by Jenifer Kitchens

Driven by Compassion 87
by Brad Simon

Learning to Cling 91
by Lisa Kibler

The Risk of Obedience 95
by Mary Holloman

The Power of Knowing

Introduction 99

Burlap Angel 100
by Dorcas Ascercion Zuniga

Squashie Detour 104
by Dawn Linton

Because I'm Convinced 108
by Mary Albers Felkins

Delectable 112
by Barb Fox

Knowing God Is with Me 116
by Jenifer Kitchens

Getting to Know You 119
by Brad Simon

Knowing That God Is Trustworthy 123
by Connie Wohlford

The Architect Knows 128
by Ron Gallagher

Knowing Our Identity 132
by Jennifer DeFrates

Can I Ask You a Personal Question? 136
by Dr. Roy E. Lucas, Jr.

The Power of Prayer

Introduction 141

The Dance of Prayer 142
by Jonathan McDuffie

Lord, Hear My Prayer 146
by Katherine Pasour

Eight Strategies for Remembering Prayer Requests 150
by Jeannie Waters

The Slow Work of God 154
by Becky Hitchcock

Save Your Amen.... 158
by J. D. Wininger

Listening for God's Voice 161
by Katy Kauffman

Prayerwalking: Praying with Compassion 165
by Krystal Weeks

White-Knuckled Urgency: The Prayer of Faith 169
by Mary Holloman

Search My Heart with Your Holiness 173
by Karen Fulgham

God's Well of Grace 175
by Billie Corley

Conclusion

Introduction 179

Home 180
by Lori Altebaumer

Contributing Authors 193
Group Discussion 201
Bibliography 203

The Power of Words
Introduction

Words are free and plentiful, but using them is a serious business. With words we wield an influence and a power for good or harm. All of us, each of us. We know from personal experience that the misuse of words stings, wounds, and burdens us, but uplifting and affirming words brighten our lives. Sometimes words can change the whole course of a life. Sometimes it's our own.

God wants us to be active and skilled in the many good uses of words. He wants us to be sentries of the words of our mouths, ambassadors that reach out to the world with the words of truth and life, encouragers that choose to bless and enrich others with words, and so on.

This section of *The Power to Make a Difference* explores the power of words. The authors give us strategies for governing our words and motivation to make it a daily habit. They help us to realize where some of our wrong words are coming from, and how to avoid them. They encourage us to feed our minds and hearts on God's good words, and to use them to squelch our negative words and to build an arsenal of good ones.

In the multitude of words sin is not lacking,
But he who restrains his lips is wise.
(Proverbs 10:19 NKJV)

Treasured Words
by Jeannie Waters

Shortly after my dad died, I discovered a treasure on the storage closet shelf. After lifting a rectangular item from a box and removing its tissue paper covering, I found a decades-old leather scrapbook I'd never seen before. The brittle yellowed pages were bound with a brown satin cord.

Placing my palms and fingers on each side of the cover sheet, I cautiously opened it to reveal the treasure—a collection of letters my grandmother Mamie's three sons sent to her during World War II.

What a brave and patriotic woman she was! With one son serving in the Navy and another in the Army, her remaining son requested permission to join his brothers in service. As a seventeen-year-old, he needed parental permission, which she granted.

For days, I cradled her scrapbook in my lap, mining every detail from letters written by a teenage foot soldier with round, wire-rimmed glasses and a heavy metal helmet serving in enemy territory. Not only did I notice dates and recorded events, but I learned more about the man who became my father. His correspondence offered insight into the fiber of his being.

Not willing to miss an opportunity to write home, my dad once penned a letter under a dim light bulb in the latrine, his words echoing love for his family and resolve to serve his country.

From Germany, he told of serving as a scout for his company, traveling ahead to ensure their safety.

Without this scrapbook's treasures, I would have missed further insight into my dad's character and how it influenced his life and mine. I now understand why he raised my brothers and me to honor God, love our country, and obey those who cared for us.

Reading his words enabled me to see him with a new lens. He was a seventeen-year-old Army private who observed the horrors of war because of patriotism, a devoted son who spared his parents additional worry by writing frequently, a brave soldier who traveled alone to ensure the safety of his company, a scared teenager who carried a small devotional in the breast pocket of his uniform, and a young man who thanked God that he and his brothers safely returned to US soil. In my book, he was a hero.

On the fifteenth of February, 1970, when I accepted Jesus as my Savior, I received another collection of treasured letters—a new Bible. I took it to school and church, and on long car rides with my family. Eager to learn more about my heavenly Father, I read it in the morning and at night, underlining verses and memorizing passages. Do you remember treasuring a new Bible?

The writer who penned the following words recognized the worth of the Scriptures. He addressed God as he declared, "I rejoice at Your word as one who finds great treasure" (Psalm 119:162 NKJV).

How did the psalmist come to value Yahweh's communication with His people? Let's look for clues in this verse that will help us embrace the riches in God's Word.

I rejoice ...

Evidently, the psalmist positioned himself not only to hear or read the sacred words personally, but he allowed the power of its truths to touch his heart. Perhaps he marveled that the Creator would communicate with man, but he spoke of a personal connection. The cherished words sparked joy in his soul and led the writer to exclaim praise.

When we set aside time to hear from God through His Word, His Spirit massages truths into our hearts so that we can rejoice. The power of God's words must have changed the psalmist, and as a result, his internal jubilance burst forth in worship. May their power do the same for us.

... at Your word ...

This writer clearly did not consider the Scripture as a once-a-week reading assignment or irrelevant language meant for others. Rather, he placed such high value on the words that he acknowledged God as their Source and expressed his amazement at the heaven-to-earth communication prize he'd experienced. Can you picture him possibly stretching out his arms while gazing at a star-filled night and exclaiming his amazement at Yahweh's recorded words? His proclamation must have brought joy to the heart of God.

... as one who finds great treasure.

When the writer penned Psalm 119:162, he had surely heard or read God's word before, but this time, its power must have settled into the depths of his heart. He labeled the collection of heavenly words a treasure, a precious possession. The psalmist must have understood a truth we read in the New Testament: "All Scripture is given by inspiration of God, and is profitable for doctrine, for reproof, for correction, for instruction in righteousness" (2 Timothy 3:16 NKJV). May we cherish the words from our heavenly Father in a renewed way.

Four Ways to Treasure God's Word

Dedicate time.

> Whether you're an early bird or a night owl, designate a time to learn more about God's character and to seek His guidance through Bible study. Consider the time as a daily

appointment with the Author of the letter you're reading, and ask Him to teach you as you read and pray.

Discover its value.

Post verses on your mirror or desk and memorize them. Watch for the ways the Holy Spirit calls them to mind when you need them for comfort, correction, and guidance.

Delight in the words of God.

Reading some of the psalms as prayers is an effective way to worship and praise God when you begin your time together. When the Lord applies specific verses to your life, record those personal messages in a journal for future reflection. Ask Him to show you passages to pray for yourself and others and to lead you to a group study.

Declare the truth and power of Scripture.

Speak Bible verses to yourself and allow them to serve as your sword in spiritual battles. As our example, Jesus used God's words to fight Satan when He was tempted (Matthew 4:1-11). As God leads, share His words with others who need encouragement or a word of witness.

The Bible, God's inspired Word, is a tried-and-tested scrapbook of treasured words, yet it is relevant to our twenty-first century lives. Consider it a personal letter from God, and ask the Holy Spirit to use the power and wonder of its contents to reveal the character of God and His plan for your life. A treasure indeed!

Prayer:

Heavenly Father, Like the psalmist, we rejoice that You speak to us through the Bible. Use the power of Your words to transform us that we will love and serve You more. In the name of Jesus, we pray. Amen.

Questions:

1. According to this study, why may the psalmist have treasured the Word of God?

2. Which Bible verses have become a treasure to you?

3. How have those verses been valuable to you in daily life?

4. Which of these verses have you memorized, or you would like to?

5. According to the following verses, why is the Word of God our treasure?
   a. Psalm 119:11
   b. Psalm 119:133
   c. Luke 11:28
   d. John 5:24
   e. John 17:17
   f. 1 Peter 2:2

Speak Life
by Krystal Weeks

Can our words speak life or death? Yes! Explosive, thoughtless words can wreak havoc. When I was thirteen, my father disciplined me and told me, "Go to your room." I shouted back, "I hate you!" as I ran from the room. I did not know at the time, that two years later from his death bed, he would say to me, "You don't really love this old man, do you?" "I do love you, Daddy," I replied softly. That was a long time ago, but I have never forgotten it. My words spoken in anger had cut deeply. I still must pray as David did, "Let the words of my mouth and the meditation of my heart be acceptable in your sight, O LORD, my rock and my redeemer" (Psalm 19:14 ESV).

Demeaning, detrimental words are as powerful as dynamite. They shape our beliefs, drive our behavior, and can devastate our lives. *Dynamite* comes from the Greek word for power. Just like dynamite, vengeful, toxic words can detonate with explosive force, and in just seconds, they can turn our world upside down. Painful words land in our hearts and spread out like shrapnel. Cruel, thoughtless words can never be taken back. They may be forgiven, but they can never be forgotten. The damage is done, and the scars remain. They can destroy relationships.

So how can we speak life through our words? How can we take the heavy load of anxiety created by hateful remarks and promulgate good words to lift hearts? "Anxiety in a man's heart weighs him down, but a good word makes him glad" (Proverbs 12:25 ESV). We can tap into God's power, and use our mouths to speak powerful, restorative words that can heal hearts. First, however, the meditations of our hearts have to be in line with God's desires, and then we can utter uplifting words. "You have a talent for …," "Thank you for going the extra mile …," "I admire the way you …," "Your support means so much …," "I really appreciate how I can always count on you …," and "Your effort and persistence are astounding …" are just a few of the examples of words that validate.

A delightful and timely word can bring energy back into our hearts and lift the weight of our burdens. Mark Twain once said, "I can live for two months on a good compliment."[1] Praise enlivens us and causes us to stand up straighter, hold our heads up higher, and walk taller.

Doris, our church Outreach Leader, is a wonderful example of someone who edifies with her every word. She's ninety years old now and a former principal. When she makes a request, you cannot say no because her words give you the confidence to complete any task. She builds you up spiritually and emotionally. I've never heard her say anything negative about anyone. All of the commendations she, herself, has received have never kept her from affirming everyone she meets. She catches people serving well and commends them for their efforts.

How did she acquire this wisdom concerning the power of positive words? She told me her mother said, "Doris, always remember to treat people like you would like to be treated."

"I know how I felt when people treated me badly," Doris added. "When you appreciate others, it makes you happy," she reminded me.

Can we emulate Doris' powerful words? We can, but first we must examine our message. We must be consciously aware of every syllable we utter. We must drop our negativity, and give thanks for the opportunity to make a difference with our words. Instead of belittling, painful words, ours can be uplifting and healing. What words are acceptable in God's eyes? What words can we use that make those around us "glad"? What types of words can we use that will revitalize hurting hearts?

Encouraging words lift our spirits. *Encourage* means "to inspire with courage, spirit, or hope."[2] Words of encouragement spur others on to use their latent potential to achieve greater goals than they had ever imagined. Whenever we walk through a lonely, difficult season, God will answer our plea of "God, please send someone to let me know You care." Invariably we will receive a call or note from someone who has empathy and loving concern for us. Words *do* have the power to breathe life back into our souls.

Affirming words validate us. They illicit a big "Yes," and confirm that we are truly appreciated for who we are. They inspire confidence. They empower us to face the world. We can shout out, "I am proud to be me." We hear from others, "You are valued."

Comforting words warm our hearts. When our hearts are breaking, and we are filled with grief, God says, "I will comfort you." And we cry out, "May your unfailing love be my comfort" (Psalm 119:76 NIV). He sends soft and comforting words through compassionate, sympathetic friends and family whose words ease the pain.

Sunny words bring a smile to our faces. They brighten our day. They lighten our mood and create a ray of hope in our darkness. When someone says, "I'm so happy to see you," it makes us feel loved. An exuberant child jabbering about his new toy makes our day worth living. Joyful words of a song make us want to worship and lift our hands in praise to God.

Loving words complete us. God is love, and He sent His Son, the Word, to speak life and love to us. We feel treasured when we are loved. "I love you" in its true form is God's love spoken through our words.

Words are powerful! Our callous, spiteful words can be heartrending, but we *can* speak life through words of love. We can emulate others who speak positive, uplifting words with liberality. Using Christ's example of breathing life into hearts by His loving words of grace, should be our mission. We can use God's powerful words to encourage, affirm, comfort, and spread joy and love to everyone we meet.

Prayer:

Father God, Forgive me for my outspoken, thoughtless words that cut and rend hearts. Only You can tame the tongue, so set a guard over my mouth. Remind me to use my lips to speak comforting, affirming words. When I see someone weighed down with anxiety and pain, please help me to speak life and love to them using Your powerful words.

Questions:

1. How has your life been affected by words you have heard or spoken?

2. What kind of words did you use today? What words should we use that will be acceptable to God?

3. Do you know someone who speaks words of gladness? How can you emulate them?

---

1. https://www.brainyquote.com/quotes/mark_twain_1003581.
2. Merriam-Webster Online, s. v. "encourage," https://www.merriam-webster.com/dictionary/encourage.

Weaponizing the Dictionary
by Ron Gallagher

Words present a unique and challenging paradox. While they are sometimes profound in their strength, at other times, when called upon to express something deeply moving, they prove themselves to be almost insulting in their impotence. Words can be treated as vitally important or considered as little more than the garnish on a plate, valued for appearance but never intended to nourish the recipient.

The Scope and Power of Words ~

The scope of territory that words can encompass and the power they can wield are immense. They can lay hold of concepts as expansive as the universe itself and expose them in ways that fill us with inexpressible awe. In many cases, words define the difference between hope and despair, establishing the basis for who will live and who will die. Words have served as tools by which men have awakened the passions and strengthened the resolve needed to rise up and carve nations out of chaos. But at other times, words have become a malignant virus that so undermined the foundations and weakened the spirit of a people that nations, once great and powerful, descended into chaos.

Given their potential for either beneficial or aggressive application, perhaps we should handle our words with the same care we use when handling weapons. Firearms, for example, are simply "unbiased" devices with no will of their own. Guns are as willing to serve the murderous gangster as they are the protective police officer or the private citizen defending his or her home. Guns bring the same capacity to do good or evil through the hands of whomever holds them. Guns also have other uses, such as hunting wildlife to provide food, or for competitive contests and personal recreation sports like skeet shooting. Guns come in all kinds, sizes, shapes, and power potential and can be configured for applications ranging from military combat to Olympic competition.

A Point of Agreement ~

Both those who love guns and those who hate them generally agree on at least one point. With their unquestioned power to project destructive force, to handle them with frivolous disregard for their potential would be foolishly irresponsible. Words that men have unleashed on one another have left a trail of violence, bloodshed, and human debris that all the guns ever made cannot equal. The Scriptures have warned us repeatedly that the words we so easily speak can become weapons that carry the same kind of painful potential.

> *The words of his mouth were smoother than butter, but war was in his heart; his words were softer than oil, yet they were drawn swords.* (Psalm 55:21 NKJV®)

> *My soul is among lions; I lie among the sons of men who are set on fire, whose teeth are spears and arrows, and their tongue a sharp sword.* (Psalm 57:4)

> *Hide me from the secret plots of the wicked, from the rebellion of the workers of iniquity, who sharpen their tongue like a sword, and bend their bows to shoot their arrows—bitter words, that they may shoot in secret at the blameless; suddenly they shoot at him and do not fear.* (Psalm 64:2-4)

We don't usually think of our dictionary as an arsenal full of potential weapons, but we might think differently if we revisit a confrontation that took place in the very beginning of our long and bloody history. When the devil invaded the Garden of Eden, intent upon destroying all of humanity, he carried no physical weapon. He had nothing with which to threaten Eve with physical harm. Instead, he confronted the "mother of all living" with the only weapon he needed—words. He assaulted her with words that first questioned, and then contradicted, the words that her Creator and Provider had spoken. Eve embraced the rebellious ideas that the devil's words conveyed and then took his weaponized sentences to her husband. She convinced him to accept them as she had done, and to eat the forbidden fruit. When he did, the human race appeared doomed forever. But thankfully, there were more powerful words yet to come and God soon revealed that the devil didn't own the dictionary.

The Word that Overcomes ~

Satan may have claimed victory as he ushered death into God's perfect world, but he surely must have trembled as a baby's cry rose up from a stable in Bethlehem. The lies, the deceitful "words," that led to the sins that filled the world with pain and death were doomed as *Grace and Truth* came to life in that stable. As air found its way into sinless human lungs, the omnipotent Word of God "became flesh and dwelt among us" (John 1:14). Satan's lies were defeated forever on Calvary's cross, and an empty tomb validated the promise Jesus made to us all in the words He spoke to Martha,

> *I am the resurrection and the life. He who believes in Me, though he may die, he shall live. And whoever lives and believes in Me shall never die.* (John 11:25-26)

Faith alone stands as the basis for our personal redemption and our means of overcoming the relentless encroachment of the world's value system. God refers us to two things that provide the unshakeable foundation for that faith, the deeds He has done and the words He has spoken. As Jesus declared to Phillip,

> *Believe Me that I am in the Father and the Father in Me, or else believe Me for the sake of the works themselves.* (John 14:11)

When Jesus had paid the awful price required for our salvation, He sent those who followed Him into the world to carry on His mission of confronting the devil's lies and contradicting ideas that pervert God's design and end in disappointment and death. He equipped those men and women and armed them for the battle with the very same weapons He used—a life empowered by His Spirit, and words that offer love, hope, healing, redemption, and restoration.

We have at our disposal a veritable dictionary full of weapons that can overcome the destructive ideas flooding our atmosphere every day. The lies and twisted philosophies that the world system promotes can only be victorious if lives that contradict them never shine, and the words that overcome them are never spoken. The dictionary is just a book until we use its contents to reveal and communicate the ideas lying dormant inside. Our Bible is just a book until we bring its words to life in ways that others can see and hear.

Prayer:

Father, Help us to handle our words with the same care that we might handle a weapon that has potential for good or harm. Let us not be frivolous or irresponsible while using them. May we receive Your powerful words and build our lives on them in ways that others can see. May we carry them forward into the world around us and nourish it with the words of eternal life and love.

Questions:

1. In Matthew 4:4, what place of importance does Jesus give the words of God?

2. According to these verses in Psalm 119, how does God's word benefit us: v.9, 11, 25, 28, 74, 93, 101, 105, 130, 133, and 165?

3. What does the arsenal of God's word in James 4:7, tell us to do about the enemy's tactics against us?

4. In 2 Kings 19:14-16, what did Hezekiah do with the enemy's words?

5. In Psalm 119:133, how can we bring the words of the Bible to life in ways that others can see and hear? In Matthew 7:24, 26?

6. What warnings does Scripture give us about the power of words in Colossians 2:4, Romans 16:18, 2 Peter 2:3, and Jude 1:16?

---

*All Scripture verses are taken from the NKJV.

Finding Strength in the Words of Life
by Connie Wohlford

"There's a strange man in my house! Please come and make him leave," my mother said over the phone.

"Okay, Mama. We'll be right over."

I had a good idea of who the man was and didn't feel that Mama was in danger. But Guy, my husband, and I went right over. My parents' home was only a quarter of a mile from our own.

We found my parents standing in the hall arguing. With a gentle voice, Daddy was saying, "Edee, you know me. I'm your husband."

She would have none of it and demanded he leave. The ravages of dementia clouded her mind. This man she fell in love with at age fifteen, married at age eighteen, raised three children with, and had shared life with for sixty-four years, was now a strange man, unwelcome in her home. She feared he was there to do her harm.

Guy and I tried to convince her that he was not a stranger, insisting he was Rudy, her husband, my father. There was no persuading her.

I whispered a plea, "Oh God, please help. Please show us what to do. Please give us the words that will help Mama understand."

Just then an idea came to me. I asked Daddy to go outside for a few minutes. Meanwhile, I hugged Mama and said, "Hello,

Mama. We came to see you," and proceeded with some small talk to redirect her thinking.

After a few minutes, Daddy came back in.

"Look, Mama. Daddy's home."

She looked at him and said, "Hi, Rudy."

Relief and gratitude rushed over my father, Guy, and me. Here was a situation where I needed the right words and the right strategy. I needed words that would bring life and light into the very dark place where my parents were struggling.

God has the right words and the right plan every time. Jesus' disciples had come to know that His words contained truth and life. But not everyone knew that.

An uncomfortable situation had arisen one day when Jesus was teaching a crowd of people. Several of Jesus' followers had turned away and left. They didn't understand the concept of Jesus' teaching. They failed to see the spiritual significance when He began to explain who He was, where He came from, and why He came.

When He told them He had come down from Heaven, they didn't get it. After all, many of them knew Him as the son of Joseph and Mary. Some had even been His childhood playmates, growing up in Nazareth.

"'Come down from Heaven?' Who does He think He is?" they mumbled.

They had seen Jesus heal sick people, and they had eaten bread and fish He miraculously provided just a couple of days before. With His power and influence, their hope was that He would be the political champion who would lead the Jews out from under the oppression of the Roman Empire. They were eager to follow a strong political leader who would not back down from the strong arm of the emperor across the Great Sea.

People gathered to hear Him teach in the Capernaum synagogue, but when He said, "I am the bread of life" (John 6:48 NKJV), eyebrows were raised. When He went on to say that one must eat His flesh and drink His blood in order to have eternal life, that was it. To some, He had crossed the line into the absurd and even the repulsive.

God's laws forbade the eating of human flesh and the drinking of blood from any source (Leviticus 3:17, Lev 17:13-14). Yet, God's laws established the sacrificial system with blood being the means of atonement for sin (Lev 17:11). Without the shedding of blood there's no remission of sins (Hebrews 9:22).

So some of Jesus' followers were puzzled by His words and didn't stick around any longer to try to understand. They had no idea Jesus was pointing to the future sacrifice of His flesh on the cross and the shedding of His blood for the remission of the sin of mankind. Offended and confused, they chose to move on.

> Then Jesus said to the twelve, "Do you also want to go away?" But Simon Peter answered Him, "Lord, to whom shall we go? You have the words of eternal life. Also we have come to believe and know that You are the Christ, the Son of the living God." (John 6:67-69 NKJV)

Words. Jesus had the right words—"the words of eternal life." Every word Jesus spoke contained life.

As spokesman for the disciples, Peter confessed the hope and future they found in their leader and teacher. Jesus spoke words that reached into eternity. Where else would they go? Who else would they follow? Only Jesus had the words of eternal life, and they were confident of that.

Jesus' words connect Earth with Heaven, mortal with immortal, the here and now with eternity. The human spirit yearns for something more—something that transcends the fall of Adam and Eve. In Jesus we find it—only in Jesus. After all, He has the words of eternal life, just as Peter stated. Think of it, life with a capital "L"—love, goodness, hope, and peace that lasts forever and ever and cannot be taken away.

Jesus said, "I am the way, the truth, and the life. No one comes to the Father except through Me" (John 14:6 NKJV). He assured His followers saying, "Lo, I am with you always, even to the end of the age" (Matthew 28:20 NASB).

God has placed eternity into the heart of every person (Ecclesiastes 3:11). Each of us has a sense that there's something beyond this life on earth, with its brevity and limitations. It's true that some say they don't believe that, but if God led Solomon to write it in his book, then that's the way it is.

Like Peter and the other disciples, we can know and confess that Jesus is the Christ. And as the first century followers did, we can hear and know His words. We have the Word of God—our Bibles—and we have the Holy Spirit and Jesus Himself, living in us, comforting us, and speaking to us.

He is well able to speak living words that encourage and instruct us. Where else would *we* go? Jesus is the One who has the words of eternal life. And we are instructed and empowered to share those words with others. We can help them understand. How amazing, that we—mere mortals—can speak words of eternal life. The eternal destiny of another person may be depending on our willingness to step out and speak Jesus' words to them. Let's learn His words and be ready to share them when opportunities arise. Let us be like His early disciples and boldly proclaim the Good News of the Gospel to others. They may not yet know that God has placed eternity in their hearts. They may not realize who He really is.

Prayer:

Father God, Thank You for Jesus. And thank You for sending Him to give us the words of eternal life. Your love and grace are beyond understanding, and we're so grateful. Help us, oh Lord, to share Your words of life with others. In Jesus' name we pray—Amen.

Questions:

1. Can you think of a time when God gave you the right words to speak in a difficult situation?

2. Do you need the right words to speak in a life situation right now? If so, ask God to give them to you and listen for His answer.

3. Why were some Jews looking for a political leader, and why was Jesus a disappointment to them?

4. Have you ever been disappointed that God answered your prayer in a way you did not prefer? Explain.

5. If your answer to question four is yes, did you eventually come around to seeing the situation God's way and how did you come to this conclusion?

6. In your own words, explain the phrase, "words of eternal life."

7. With whom have you shared the living words of Jesus?

Silence Negative Self-Talk: Go Beyond the Inner Critic

by K. A. Wypych

My life changed when I became a runner.

Despite the immense health benefits of exercise, the biggest draw of running for me was so I could outrun my inner critic.

How can we overcome this? Let's look at three examples.

1. "You're not good enough."

I don't have to worry about being "good enough" because Jesus was good enough in my place. Hallelujah! And, because of His sacrifice, I know with certainty that I am loved beyond all limits (a love I could never deserve and which will never wane).

Reading God's Word on a daily basis is a good start to fortifying a foundation based on God's love. It may seem like an oversimplified solution, however, the benefit is real. No one learns Spanish by practicing once a year or even once a week. You have to be "in" the topic to absorb and understand it.

When you spend time in the Bible, focus on what God says about His children. Highlight any area you come across which speaks about who God says you are. Or better yet, memorize a few key verses. When you feel your negative critic coming to life, go back and read the highlighted verses. Contrary to how you may feel, the critic isn't right. God loves His children, and He always will.

> *For I am sure that neither death nor life, nor angels nor rulers, nor things present nor things to come, nor powers, nor height nor depth, nor anything else in all creation, will be able to separate us from the love of God in Christ Jesus our Lord.* (Romans 8:38-39 ESV)

2. "Your thighs are too fat."

Comparison is death. Now, I may have big thighs (as I said, I'm an endurance runner), but compared to whom? Who sets the standard? God? I never found that passage in the Bible.

Do you want to tone down negative self-talk? Then maybe we need to limit what we put in front of our faces. Social media and television paint unrealistic pictures of what we should look like and who we should strive to be.

Take an Instagram holiday for a month, choosing to read inspirational books or even fiction. There are other ways to "veg out" without feeding the critic. Substitute a useful and practical TV show for The Bachelor (you get the idea).

> *So God created man in his own image, in the image of God he created him; male and female he created them.* (Genesis 1:27 ESV)

3. "You shouldn't have said that. You sounded stupid."

Why, oh, why do we care so much about what others think? A lot of negative self-talk comes from imagining what others think about us. If I put forth the effort into my writing craft that I do into worrying about what others think, I'd have published a dozen books by now!

Listen, people will love you or they won't. Basing how you feel about yourself on how others treat you is a recipe for disaster. People are fallible. Honestly, "they" are probably too busy worrying about how "they" look to think about you at all.

Spend time noticing your strengths, and make a list in a journal. Even if you can only find a few things you like about yourself (it gets easier over time), write those down and say a prayer of thanks. Do this on a daily basis to grow your positive self-talk.

The fear of man lays a snare, but whoever trusts in the Lord is safe. (Proverbs 29:25 ESV)

Here are a couple of things to remember. First, God loves you and sees your innate value. Second, to silence negative self-talk and grow a positive inner monologue, we need to be intentional about what we feed our minds and which thoughts we choose to dwell on. It takes practice, and it won't happen overnight. But, you are worthy. You are beautiful. You have great value. Take some time to discover what God already sees in you.

Prayer:

Dear Lord, Through our personal sin nature and the sin nature of the world, I've developed a skewed view of who You created me to be. Please show me who I am to You. Reveal how You see me, Father. Help me to stand up in who You've called me to be; give me the strength and the vision to be accountable yet shame free. Be present in my life and help me to continually rely on You when my negative self-talk rears its head. I pray this in Jesus' name. Amen.

Questions:

1. In your quiet time, think about your most common negative self-talk comments. Where is your greatest area of struggle?

2. What kinds of events or remarks aggravate and escalate that struggle?

3. Which verses in God's word silence the negative self-talk and give you peace in that area?

4. Take a moment to read Psalm 139.
    a. What does it mean in v.14 (NKJV) to be "fearfully and wonderfully made"?
    b. How does that reflect on our Creator?
    c. How should it help our self-talk?

5. God views His children as "joint heirs with Christ" (Romans 8:17 NKJV). How does this compare and contrast with your view of self?

Wonderful Words of Life
by Karen O. Allen

Following my testimony at church, Cindy called one Sunday night to inquire about the Bible study I had written, *Confronting Cancer with Faith*, thinking it might help her mom. I knew Cindy from church because her name was on the prayer list. She was dealing with a vascular problem in which she almost lost her leg. In the midst of the conversation I learned Cindy was also dealing with something else: childlessness. Infertility was not the issue; she had experienced two miscarriages. She was told her autoimmune disorder would make it difficult to carry a child to full-term, yet she persevered only to discover the doctors were right.

Children of God

The thought of Hannah and Sarah in the Bible crossed my mind while talking with my new friend. Both barren women traveled the same hopeful path. Both women loved the Lord and appealed for His mercy, and both women were ridiculed for their childlessness.

Hannah was a woman of grace and devout prayer. Her experience and the scorn from her husband's second wife Peninnah, who boasted of her children, helped mold Hannah's character and faith. She vowed to give God back the thing she wanted most: a child (1 Samuel 1:9-11). God answered her prayer and granted her a son who would become a great judge and prophet.

Sarah would become the mother to the Jewish nation (Isaiah 51:2). Her pregnancy was delayed so that the glory of God could be exalted, but Sarah wasn't concerned about God's glory like Hannah.

Sarah wanted to build a family with Abraham (Genesis 16:2). She knew of God's promise to her husband to make him into a great nation (Genesis 12:2), but she had not been specifically identified as the mother of that great nation (though it could be assumed). Maybe God had other plans. So she gave her Egyptian slave to her husband as a wife, which was legal in that day. Hagar conceived and bore a son, but this was not God's plan. How many times do we get ahead of ourselves trying to rush God's plan?

Unlike Hannah, Sarah showed impatience, disobedience, and distrust. She laughed at the possibility of conception at her advanced age. Her doubtful response prompted God to ask her husband, "Is anything impossible for the LORD?" (Genesis 18:14 HCSB). I found myself asking Cindy the same question. The Bible answers it—"Nothing will be impossible with God" (Luke 1:37 HCSB)—but do we believe God will do the impossible for *us*?

God's Ways, God's Timing

Cindy and I became fast friends and spent hours on the phone. On one occasion I told her I felt the Lord wanted her to be a mother. *How could I say such compelling words?* Because they weren't just words; I believed them. I believed God's plan included a child for my friend.

When Cindy called to say she was pregnant again, we were ecstatic and celebrated over lunch on the day of her ultrasound. This new life seemed to be the answer to our prayers.

For the next several months, Cindy called to give periodic updates and to thank me for my prayers and encouragement. Then one evening she called to say she had lost the baby. A third miscarriage. I cringed when she thanked me for allowing her to fall in love with this unborn child. We cried together and wondered how this could happen. Still, I couldn't shake the idea that God wanted Cindy to be a mother.

"You *will* be a mother," I said.

Adoption seemed to be the next logical step. Cindy and Scott decided to resurrect the notion they had previously pursued with skepticism. All was proceeding painstakingly slowly including a home visit, when Cindy received devastating news: she might have breast cancer. Adoption seemed out of the question. Options were exhausted. Maybe it wasn't cancer. I maintained my confidence and conviction for motherhood but prayed with fervor that Cindy's biopsy results would be negative. This was not to be the case. *What now, God?*

I reminded Cindy (and myself) that God can do the impossible. I was surprised at the empowerment and demonstration of faith from my words. They were exactly what she needed to hear. I realized what I had said and hoped I had not projected a false sense of optimism. *So what if I had? Was that so bad?* God's Word is Truth, and I was verbalizing my faith to lean upon its promises.

Later that night I retreated for some heart-to-heart abandoned prayer time. I pleaded with God to give the Darnell's a child somehow, someway. In my heart I felt it would happen but had no idea how. I didn't have to!

Cindy and Scott withdrew advancements towards adoption, allowing Cindy's health to take priority. She opted for a mastectomy with reconstruction and had the surgery in the hospital where she worked as a Labor and Delivery nurse.

A few days later I received a phone call at work. Scott's message was short and energized.

"Pray, pray, pray," he said.

A young woman had come into the hospital emergency room about to deliver and inquired if there was anyone that wanted a baby. One of the employees from Labor and Delivery was quick to answer.

"Yes, I know someone," she said.

She contacted Cindy who was still an inpatient. Of course, she was interested. *Could this be the miracle, the impossible thing we'd been waiting for?* Yes, yes it was. It was indeed. Who could have imagined such an incredible, remarkable, unmistakable God thing?

I came back to the hospital the next day to meet Miles Morrison Darnell. A few weeks later I attended his adoption at the courthouse. Birthday parties and Christmases have come and gone as I've watched Miles grow into a handsome young man. He looks nothing like his parents but has the smile of God upon his life.

Beautiful words, wonderful words, wonderful words of life (refrain from the hymn "Wonderful Words of Life" by Philip Bliss) were used to speak life into a difficult situation. We know God does not call for all married women to have children, but God does call each of us to trust Him. Completely and wholly and at all times. Are you able to trust Him and His ways in your life?

Prayer:

Dear Father, Your Word is true; however, sometimes we have a difficult time leaning on Your promises in the midst of our circumstances. Help us, Lord, call upon You and trust in Your ways to do what is best for us in the plan You have. Strengthen our obedience. In Your name I pray, Amen.

Questions:

1. How did not getting what she wanted, affect Hannah? How did it affect Sarah?

2. Are you usually inclined to one or the other?

3. Have you ever come alongside someone struggling with an impossible situation? If so, what helped?

4. How does it affect our relationship with Him, when "Nothing will be impossible with God" becomes our reality?

5. How should we handle it when the impossible thing that we are hoping for, is not God's will for us?

6. What are some *wonderful words of life* spoken to you by a teacher, friend, or loved one?

The Power of Encouraging Words
by Katherine Pasour

"Atta girl! You can make it. Keep going!"

The first grader huffed out a breath, clenched her teeth and steadily continued her crunches (sit-ups) as the stop watch raced forward on its sixty-second count.

"You're almost there!" I urged, counting her repetitions as I pressed gently to hold her feet. She grunted on each upward surge as she maintained a steady rhythm of up and down.

"Stop! Times up." I shut off the watch.

She collapsed onto her back, but immediately rose again to a sitting position, eyes aglow with fierce anticipation. "Did I get enough?"

"Yes." I smiled as her face lit up like a burst of sunlight following a summer rainstorm.

"My Daddy's going to be so proud!" She jumped to her feet, gave me a hug, and sped back to her classroom.

Carrie* qualified for the President's Challenge Physical Fitness Award. This hard-working, highly motivated student had previously breezed through the mile run, flexibility test, pull-ups, and shuttle run, scoring above the 85th percentile.

But sit-ups had defeated her.

Encouragement (giving support, offering confidence and hope) made the difference for Carrie. This sweet creation of God received a second chance, and her willingness to try again brought success to this determined six-year-old.

Therefore encourage one another and build each other up, just as in fact you are doing. (1 Thessalonians 5:11 NIV)**

Our words are powerful. And most certainly, words of parents, teachers, and extended family wield tremendous force as we encourage (or discourage) our children. Little ones thrive on affirmation of their achievements and recognition of milestones of growth. Setting challenges suitable to the child's age and abilities and providing positive feedback, fosters further learning and leads to healthy intrinsic motivation (from within) to succeed.

Encouragement is not limited to children; we have ample opportunities to encourage (or discourage) our family, friends, and co-workers on a regular basis. Affirmation for a job well done or encouragement for ongoing attempts impacts how we grow, develop, and succeed.

Encouragement builds positive self-esteem and the confidence and initiative to keep trying. Children and adults thrive on positive reinforcement or, as the Apostle Paul would say, "build each other up."

But what if we're not encouraged?

My earthly father was often harsh, demanding, and critical. His verbal attacks pumped fear into the hearts of his children and robbed them of self-confidence. He was *not* an encourager.

Perhaps his parenting style was a carryover from his own father. My dad lived through the depression and survived the European Campaign of World War II. He had demons of his own to deal with. I suppose that he loved me, but he didn't know how to show it. As a result, I became an overachiever, a perfectionist, impatient with my own weaknesses and those of others. My ability to be an encouraging teacher, wife, parent, and friend is the result of my mother's love and God's grace in healing me from the lingering pain of my father's verbal discouragement.

Words of discouragement are powerful in shaping our sense of who we are. Excessive negative verbal feedback can cause fear, anxiety, depression, and hopelessness. The Word of God is firm about negative behaviors we should avoid.

> **Get rid of all bitterness, rage and anger, brawling and slander, along with every form of malice. Be kind and compassionate to one another, forgiving each other, just as in Christ God forgave you. (Ephesians 4:31-32)**

If we avoid malice and slander and are kind and compassionate in our verbal and non-verbal communication (body language), then we will be encouragers.

The Psalmist reminds us that using our words for good is in accordance to God's will. Our verbal interactions with (or about) others should be positive. We should avoid words which might cause harm.

> **Whoever of you loves life and desires to see many good days, keep your tongue from evil and your lips from telling lies. Turn from evil and do good; seek peace and pursue it. The eyes of the LORD are on the righteous, and his ears are attentive to their cry; but the face of the LORD is against those who do evil, to blot out their name from the earth. (Psalm 34:12-16)**

Jesus provides a positive role model for us. He often took on the role of teacher and mentor in His ministry. Our Lord demonstrated the importance of encouragement in His relationship with His disciples. His living example and guidance during His time on Earth enabled the apostles to carry on the work of spreading the Gospel after Jesus ascended into heaven.

> **Then Jesus came to them and said, "All authority in heaven and on earth has been given to me. Therefore go and make disciples of all nations, baptizing them in the name of the**

Father and of the Son and of the Holy Spirit, and teaching them to obey everything I have commanded you. And surely I am with you always, to the very end of the age." (Matthew 28:18-20)

Jesus reminded His disciples (and we are included) that *He is always with us*. Through His teaching, encouragement, and confidence in His disciples, Christ equipped them **"for works of service, so that the body of Christ may be built up until we all reach unity in the faith and in the knowledge of the Son of God and become mature, attaining to the whole measure of the fullness of Christ" (Ephesians 4:12-13)**.

Encouraging our children, family, fellow church members, colleagues, and peers builds them up to work for our Lord. Our words of affirmation, support, and encouragement spread the Good News of Jesus Christ and influence others to live as children of God.

My young student grew into a confident, well-adjusted, wonderful young lady. She flourished in academics and athletics. She served many years as a teacher and now has children of her own.

I cannot take credit for her success, but I know the power of words, as utilized by teachers and parents, contributes significantly to the development of our children. I believe that our words and actions, *in all cases*, have tremendous impact on others. I will always remember Carrie's joy when she successfully achieved the fitness goal she had set for herself. She wanted to please her earthly father—and she did. Now Carrie pleases her heavenly Father as she serves as a positive and encouraging role model in her church, to her own children, and to others.

I believe our Father is proud of her.

As children of God, is our heavenly Father proud of us for our positive and encouraging attitude? Are we using the power of our words and actions to encourage others in their walk with Christ?

Prayer:

Father, I know I've been guilty of using my words inappropriately. Sometimes, I've **discouraged** Your children rather than **encouraged**. I pray as the Psalmist did: *May these words of my mouth and this meditation of my heart be pleasing in your sight, LORD, my Rock and my Redeemer* (Psalm 19:14). Lord, please guide me to be an encourager in my words and actions, that I may serve You by serving Your children. In the precious name of Jesus, Amen.

Questions:

1. The Apostle Paul emphasizes the importance of building up one another (2 Corinthians 10:8 and 13:10; Ephesians 4:12). Building up can be considered encouragement. What does building up look like in action? What specific words and actions have you found to be the most encouraging to others?

2. The opposite of building up can come in many forms. Using the guidelines of Ephesians 4:31-32 and other Scriptural guidance, what are the behaviors that we should avoid in order to avoid being the perpetrator of discouragement?

3. Our children, grandchildren, and peers are strongly impacted by our words and examples. How can we model encouragement for them? Since none of us are perfect, how can we let those who are watching, learn from our mistakes?

4. Proverbs 12:25 reminds us that—"**Anxiety weighs down the heart, but a kind word cheers it up.**" What strategies can we use to encourage and cheer others when they are anxious and afraid? Can you share an example of when someone encouraged you? Or how you have encouraged others?

5. "**And we know that in all things God works for the good of those who love him, who have been called according to his**

purpose" (Romans 8:28). How does sharing encouragement in a loving manner to others fit into God's purpose for us?

*Note: Carrie is not her real name.
**All Scripture verses are taken from the NIV.

Are Your Words Fitly Spoken?
by Dorcas Asercion Zuniga

"Can you say something to make me feel better?"

My baby sister would always ask me that whenever she was going through a rough time. So we would have a sister-to-sister, heart-to-heart session that would end up with both of us feeling comforted and loved.

It's amazing how the right words, at just the right time, can make all the difference in a person's day—or even life.

Such was the case for my mother. She had left her home country, the Philippines, with three young children to join my dad in the United States. With no family nearby, she was desperately homesick. She told us about those days when we got older and about the physician who treated her. She said just talking to him made her feel better. His care and compassion healed the underlying cause of her physical ailments—her lonely heart.

"Anxiety weighs down the heart, but a kind word cheers it up." (Proverbs 12:25 NIV[*])

Solomon writes about the right words spoken at the right time: "A word fitly spoken is like apples of gold in settings of silver" (Proverbs 25:11 NKJV).

By definition, "fitly" is an adverb that means "in a fit manner; at the right time."[1] A fitly spoken word is suitable[2] for the occasion. Such a word is as beautiful as golden apples in a silver basket.

Our Savior Yeshua** was Master of the spoken word. For every circumstance, He knew what to say and how to say it, in order to get the attention of His listeners.

"All spoke well of him and were amazed at the gracious words that came from his lips" (Luke 4:22). "They were amazed at his teaching, because his words had authority" (Luke 4:32).

Words are powerful. How they are used determines what type of impact they make.

Most of us grew up reciting variations of the expression, "Sticks and stones will break my bones, but words will never harm me." This saying is meant to empower children to rise above hurtful remarks made against them. But the fact is, words do hurt. However, the right words can do the opposite.

Words can heal.

"Gracious words are a honeycomb, sweet to the soul and healing to the bones." (Proverbs 16:24)

Throughout history, honey has been used for medicinal purposes in many cultures, and modern science has confirmed the great benefits of this sweet golden liquid. Among its many properties is its ability to heal wounds and burns.[3] So it is no wonder that Solomon likens gracious words—words that are "courteous, kind, and pleasant"[4]—to the honeycomb. Where hurtful words can "break," kind words can heal.

Many times I walk into an exam room to be greeted by hurting souls. After lots of tissues and hand-holding, words of reassurance, and often times, prayers, the quivering lips turn into smiles. My patients would offer words like, "I knew I would feel better after talking to you," or "Thank you so much; you always know what to say." Each time this happens, I think back to my mother and her physician from long ago. I am humbled and blessed to be used as an instrument of Divine comfort.

In the book of Matthew, Yeshua spoke, and the centurion's servant was healed (Matthew 8:5-13). Through the power of His words, the paralyzed man was able to walk (Matthew 9:2-8). Our words may not bring about physical healing, but, through the grace of the Great Physician, they can help mend broken hearts.

Words can encourage.

"Therefore encourage one another and build each other up, just as in fact you are doing." (1 Thessalonians 5:11)

I was painfully shy and insecure in middle school. During one English class in ninth grade, our teacher placed cards with different adjectives around the room. She told us to go to the card that we felt best described us. Another student and I stood in the corner labeled "timid." Our teacher silenced the laughter aimed at us and spoke of the beauty and value of a quiet, gentle soul. Her words of encouragement throughout that year laid down the stepping stones for me to venture out of my comfort zone and grow.

The Apostle Paul was an outspoken defender of the Good News. His written and spoken words both advised and admonished. But his words also offered great encouragement to the early Church (Acts 20:2), and he instructed the believers to "encourage one another" (2 Corinthians 13:11). In the same loving spirit, we can also be encouragers.

Words can calm.

"A gentle answer turns away wrath, but a harsh word stirs up anger." (Proverbs 15:1)

It is truly amazing to see this Proverb in action. I'm ashamed to admit, however, that I was the one who needed that "gentle answer." I had called the customer service department to cancel a subscription for a skincare product. The young man who answered, proceeded to speak while I was speaking and insisted on offering me a special deal to continue with the product. He refused to cancel my subscription. My anger and the volume of my voice rapidly increased. Finally, he hung up on me.

Oh no! That would not do. I promptly called back. A different voice came on the line. I complained about my earlier phone encounter. The young man on the other end apologized for my inconvenience and assured me that he would cancel my subscription. I could literally feel the tension in my head and neck dissipate. He got all the necessary information and thanked me for my patience. I, in turn, thanked him for his kind assistance and hung up, totally ashamed of my behavior.

When a sudden "furious storm" (Matthew 8:24) swept over their boat, the disciples frantically awakened the sleeping Yeshua. He "got up and rebuked the winds and the waves, and it was completely calm" (Matthew 8:26). The Master of the "winds and the waves" will give us the right words to calm an angry soul—and that power can come through gentle words.

> "May these words of my mouth and this meditation of my heart be pleasing in your sight, [Yahweh],* my Rock and my Redeemer." (Psalm 19:14)

If our heart's desire is to "be pleasing" to our Heavenly Father, the words that we speak will also be acceptable to Him. And through His Spirit, He will use our words to make a positive impact on those who hear them.

Prayer:

Father in Heaven, Help me to know what to say, whatever the situation, so that Your Name will be glorified. Let my words be uplifting and always pleasing to You.

Questions:

1. How have your words helped someone get through a difficult situation?

2. What advice or words of encouragement from others have spurred you to press on?

3. What advice or encouragement from Scripture has been especially meaningful and helpful to you?

4. What should guide our words and actions? (See Colossians 3:17 and 1 Corinthians 13:1.)

---

*All Bible verses are taken from the NIV translation unless otherwise noted.

**Author's Note: Yahweh is the divine name of our Heavenly Father, and Yeshua is the Hebrew name of Jesus. Thank you for letting me share these special names with you.

1. Collins Dictionary, s.v. "fitly," https://www.collinsdictionary.com/dictionary/english/fitly.
2. Ibid.
3. Joseph Nordqvist, "Everything You Need to Know about Honey," *Medical News Today*, February 14, 2018, https://www.medicalnewstoday.com/articles/264667.php.
4. Oxford Dictionaries, s. v. "gracious," https://en.oxforddictionaries.com/definition/gracious.

Hitting Pause on Words That Wound
by Lori Brown

When I reached the age of sixteen, I suddenly thought my parents knew nothing. Consequently, I became a moody and emotionally challenging teenager at times. One day I got angry with my mom. In haste, I yelled painful words, stomped down the hallway to my bedroom, and slammed the door. For the next few seconds, you could have heard a pin drop in that house, but that was only the calm before the storm. My dramatic exit was short-lived.

I could continue with the rest of the story, but let's just say that it's not very pretty. Before I could plot the next move, my mom had the bedroom door wide open and was standing at the foot of the bed with the reminder that we don't "act that way" in the Brown household.

It didn't take long to realize that my ugly words and disrespectful behaviors hurt my mother and damaged our healthy relationship. In short, I was an angry teenager who sinned and was sadly ignorant of the cost. Was trying to get my way worth the emotional pain of the damaging words I had so mercilessly thrown at my mother?

I think we can all agree that angry, hurtful, and disrespectful words have little place in the Kingdom, yet, they are frequently common, particularly in seasons of frustration. Disillusionment and hardship sometimes lead our lips and language to dark places, as it did in my childhood home almost thirty years ago.

We shouldn't be surprised to find similarly dark instances throughout the Scriptures. In fact, the New International Version includes 270 uses of the word "anger" and 115 uses of "angry." Why does this matter, you ask? Because even God's people get angry, and anger often leads to sin. I think it's fair to say that some of the Bible is a comprehensive biography of hurting people who often responded by hurting others with their weapons of words.

Let's consider some historical examples, starting with Adam and Eve.

- In Genesis 3, Adam wounded his Creator with deceitful words—"I heard the sound of You in the garden, and I was afraid because I was naked; so I hid myself" (Genesis 3:10 NASB'). Did Adam honestly believe that God was clueless?

- Adam additionally wounded Eve with accusatory and blaming words—"The man said, 'The woman whom You gave to be with me, she gave me from the tree, and I ate.'" (Genesis 3:12).

Again, did Adam really believe what he was saying? Did he honestly believe that the blame game was going to deepen his commitment to Eve? For Adam, sin led to embarrassment, which then led to deceit and a willing spirit to hurt the two persons who comprised his whole world—God and Eve. But Adam was just the first among many to act in a similar fashion. Consider:

- Peter publicly denied knowing Jesus ("Woman, I do not know Him" [Luke 22:57]).

- Elkanah's second wife, Peninnah, mercilessly teased a barren Hannah (the first wife) to the point of tears (1 Samuel 1:6-8).

- The Roman soldiers mocked Jesus and called Him names as they tortured His body before the crucifixion (Matthew 27:29-31).

In each case, the loss of power, pride, position, or priority resulted in hurting people who hurt others with their words, despite the modeled behavior of a perfect Savior who lived out the commands of Ephesians 4. This beautiful New Testament passage reminds us of ways to hit pause.

- Avoid sinning in our anger (v.26).
- Keep our speech clean (v.29).
- Watch our words (v.31).

If Jesus was able to follow these commands, how do we follow suit? Or, to put it another way, how do we hit pause on words that wound?

Ironically, the best answer to that question is found in Jesus' lack of words. As referenced in Matthew 27, when Jesus faced the greatest physical torture of His life, He uttered few words before Pilate and responded to each blow with silence. He met insults with intimate reflection and physical pain with a priestly patience.

As Jesus neared His final breath, His only words were directed toward the soul-searching criminal at Calvary and to His Holy Father. In what could have been a Hollywood-worthy scene of deep rage, Jesus chose quiet reverence.

Difficult though it may be, you and I can choose to do the same. The best way to hit pause on words that wound, is to hold the tongue while directing our conflicted hearts and souls to the Father. Instead of harsh words, we can choose His healing. Instead of deceptive words, we can choose His directives, and instead of rash thought or deed, we can choose His redemption. Give your wounding words to the Savior today and watch Him work.

Prayer:

Dear God, I come to You today asking for wisdom with my words. Sometimes I speak without realizing how painful my words may be to others. I want to honor You and reflect Your character, which means I need to exercise caution and compassion in all things. I pray for listening ears and a humble spirit so that my responses to others serve to build up rather than tear down the Kingdom. Guide me, Father God, with today's words.

Questions:

1. Have you ever been wounded by the words of others? If so, how did God help you heal from that experience?

2. Why do you think it is so difficult to listen more than we speak?

3. When you reflect on the way Jesus responded to wounding words, how does it make you feel?

4. In addition to prayer and time in the Word, can you think of practical strategies to help you hit pause before speaking painful words?

5. How does knowing that the Bible is filled with stories of hurting people, impact your relationship with God today?

---

*All Scripture verses are taken from the NASB.

Of Butter and War, Oil and Swords
by Mary Albers Felkins

I don't consider myself a violent person.

<u>Disclaimer:</u> If my stash of Peanut M&Ms® goes missing, I am known to get downright testy but never violent.

I've never considered taking anyone's life by sword, though I own a Smith & Wesson and pepper spray for purposes of self-defense. With great respect for those called to serve our country, I've never had any inkling to join the military. Aside from the study of our nation's history, I have little interest in things of war.

Tenderhearted toward the suffering, I cringe at violence. All it takes is about fifteen minutes of hearing the news and I'm out. My heart clenches and I get angry. Or sad. Why can't we all just be nice to one another and get along?

Why doesn't it start with ... me?

Scripture reveals the deceitfulness of slick and buttery words and false flattery when the heart is contemplating harm. Or worse.

Those who flatter their neighbors are spreading nets for their feet. (Proverbs 29:5 NIV®)

Are we spreading nets unaware? Worse, fully aware? Is the butter and oil of our speech a means to lure others to engage in godless warfare, the swords of our tongues drawn and ready?

The power and gift of words. By them, Jesus brought down the lofty (John 19:11), healed the sick (Matthew 8:13, plus countless other examples), silenced the storm (Mark 4:39), taught His followers (Matthew 5:1-12), and silenced the demons (Matthew 8:28-32). He always used words for the Father's glory and for our good.

What God desires in the inmost part of our soul is truth, a transformation from the inside out.

David knew this:

What you're after is truth from the inside out. (Psalm 51:6 The Message)

And out of the overflow of the heart will flow … truth. *For the mouth speaks what the heart is full of* (Matthew 12:34).

Points to Ponder:

1. Give thought to our thoughts. At some point it's likely those ramblings of our heart will spill over. Are we nursing resentment or praise? What will be the outcome if our thoughts are uttered? Will they bless or curse the receiver?

2. Maintain humility. A willingness to offer our words to God for holy editing first in order that they align with His heart will result in far better outcomes.

Take words with you and return to the LORD. Say to him, "Forgive all our sins and receive us graciously, that we may offer the fruit of our lips." (Hosea 14:2)

3. Check our motives. When we feel an overwhelming urge to say something, even a simple compliment or praise, it's a good practice to stop and ask, *"Why? What's driving the urge?"* Are we buttering up the listener for our own good? *May the LORD silence all flattering lips and every boastful tongue* (Psalm 12:3). Or are we looking to engage in verbal warfare?

Given that nothing of our hearts is hidden from Him and He's in on every conversation, let's use the gift and power of words He's entrusted us with for the good of the hearer.

Let's pray …

May these words of my [our] mouth and this meditation of my [our] heart be pleasing in your sight, LORD, my [our] Rock and my [our] Redeemer. (Psalm 19:14)

Questions:

1. Which of the Points to Ponder do you think would be the most effective in making you a good steward of the gift and power of words? Why?

2. What would it look like to apply these points at home? At work? At church? With friends? How would this be helpful?

3. Which of these Bible verses most inspires you to watch your words? To exercise humility in heated situations? To check your motives before you speak?

---

*All Scripture verses are taken from the NIV unless otherwise indicated.

The Power of Doing
Introduction

What we *do* matters. It has power. Strung together, our actions form an adventure that unfolds over a lifetime, making a staccato pattern of ordinary days and defining moments. Our initiatives and responses shape who we are and how we touch the lives of others.

What God does matters, and it has power. He works, He expresses His love in different ways, He invests. He pours His heart and soul into His children's lives, and suddenly our adventure changes. It's brighter, more meaningful, and more productive. When God invests Himself in our lives, good things happen.

This section of *The Power to Make a Difference* is full of stories, testimonies, and encouragement about some of the good things that happen when what we do is shaped, led, and blessed by what God does.

Now may our Lord Jesus Christ Himself,
and our God and Father, ...
establish you in every good word and work.
(2 Thessalonians 2:16-17 NKJV)

Overwhelmed Is a Good Place to Be
by Marilyn Nutter

*May the God of hope fill you with all joy and peace
as you trust in him,
so that you may overflow with hope
by the power of the Holy Spirit.*
(Romans 15:13 NIV)

The loud beep alerted me that the coffee was brewed. Still sleepy, I poured a cup and took a sip of warm liquid comfort. As I walked to my sunroom, my favorite spot for morning devotions, I sighed. I had a lot on my mind. Taking another sip of coffee, I thought about a family member under hospice care, another having school struggles, and a friend in a marriage crisis. In recent weeks, I've spent time with phone calls, writing cards, and texting. I hurt for others, and I've prayed and wept for them. Despite a good night's sleep, I was tired. I looked out the window and thought about the yard work that needs to be done—a big task requiring energy I didn't have. I sighed, overwhelmed.

I reached for my journal, found a pen, and began to write. Then I thought, *Overwhelmed is a good place to be.* What? A good place? As I wrote in my journal, nothing had changed, but I was beginning to sense hope. I began my L-I-S-T.

L: List each prayer request. Some were heavy, with no apparent resolution this side of heaven. Others involved people—including me—who had to take responsibility. I questioned if one or two were hopeless from a human point of view, unless people wanted to change.

I: Invite God into each one. I asked, "How can I lean into God in these situations? Romans 15:13 (NIV) says, *May the God of hope fill you with all joy and peace as you trust in him*, so what do I specifically trust in? How? Who is God in this? How do I have hope?" My job was to trust His character despite some apparently devastating and difficult circumstances. The answers came.

- He is Jehovah Shalom, the one who is peace and gives peace, even in struggles. (Judges 6:24)

- He is Jehovah-Jireh—a provider of what we need, not necessarily what we might want. (Genesis 22:14)

- He is Elohim—Creator, the One who continues to make, arrange, rearrange, and orchestrate because of His singular strength and power. (Genesis 1:1)

- He is El Roi—the One who sees everyone and everything. There is confidence knowing He sees and knows me and those I love. (Genesis 16:13)

- He is Elyon—God Most High—my sovereign, trustworthy God. (Psalm 83:18)

My hope and peace rest in the promise that God lives up to His character that is revealed by His names. I sighed—a different sigh. Not the overwhelmed sigh, but a sigh of God-confident peace. Still I knew there was more.

S: Find **Scripture** that relates to each issue. My heart was beginning to change.

- I prayed Isaiah 26:3 and asked help for myself, as well as those with heartache and disappointment, to keep our minds on Him, not circumstances, difficult people, or distractions. Jehovah Shalom will give peace.

- I prayed James 1:5 and asked for wisdom. Jehovah-Jireh will provide it.

- I moved to Psalm 138:8 and acknowledged He will fulfill His purposes. Elohim is at work.

- I read Lamentations 3:22-23 and thanked Him for His mercies and faithfulness, now and in the future. I take comfort that El Roi sees.

- I ended with Psalm 42 and put my hope in Elyon, my sovereign God.

T: Turn your list over to God. I asked Him to give me, and those I am praying for, wisdom, comfort, and peace. In each prayer, I agreed with the truth of His Word and handed God the situation or person.

I also handed Him, once more, myself. My final Scripture was Jeremiah 18:4 (NIV), *But the pot he was shaping from the clay was marred in his hands; so the potter formed it into another pot, shaping it as seemed best to him.*

God is a potter who remakes pots as it suits Him. My size and shape change according to what He wants to do with me. I'd like to think I hold more of Him and my shape changed as I prayed these Scriptures. Yes, overwhelmed is a good place to be. My new shape, as I rested and trusted, held hope, so that I, a pot, could overflow with hope by the power of the Holy Spirit.

Though life may not look like we planned, or a day may have serious life-threatening challenges, the character of God gives joy and hope as we trust Him. My concerns remain. So does my hope in God.

I looked out the window. Today my responsibility is to tackle yard work—after my second cup of coffee.

Prayer:

Father, I am in a difficult place. People and situations disappoint, and I know at times I disappoint others, causing tension. Today I pray Romans 15:13 and commit to trust You. Where I need to take responsibility, give me Your strength and courage to do so. Where I need to step back from discouragement or trying to take control, help me to do so. Your Word is truth, and I ask that You fill me with joy and hope as I trust in You. Then may the hope that I have, overflow to those around me and nourish them, so they see You. In Jesus' name, Amen.

Questions:

1. Which names of God and His character relate to your current struggle or concern? List them, then look for Scripture to correlate with each one.

    For example, if you chose Jehovah-Jireh, "The Lord will provide," Philippians 4:8 could be the related Scripture. You might consider writing verses on index cards to keep handy, or if you journal, write the verse as a prayer.

2. Romans 15:13 tells us that God will fill us with joy as we trust in Him. Look up Nehemiah 8:10. Note the difference between a change in circumstances which could promote temporary happiness versus joy in the Lord despite circumstances.

3. Look up each of the Scriptures in this study. Is there one that particularly speaks to you today?

Serving God in a Season of Brokenness
by Lori Brown

"Just pick up the phone and call them, Lori. You can do this. Stop making excuses! Pick up the phone and offer your volunteer services again."

Heavy sigh. I just kept staring at my smart phone, feeling anything but smart. This was not going well. All I had to do was call the local Rescue Mission, a faith-based homeless shelter in the heart of my city, and utter five little words: "I'm ready to volunteer again!"

The Western Carolina Rescue Mission was the place where I had previously put feet to my faith and engaged in volunteer missions. In the height of my faithfulness, I regularly visited homeless women and their children, sharing devotions, praying together, and laughing over some sort of sinful sweet treat!

But with the stress of life and the pull of worldly pleasure, I lost sight of doing this good work, pulled away, and invested in landing my "dream job"—the job that signaled that I had "made it."

But my self-absorbed victory was short-lived. Only sixteen months after starting a dream job offering a super sweet six-figure salary, conditions turned ugly and I heard those painful words that every employee fears: "Due to budget cutbacks, we're eliminating your position. You're done today." Serenity turned to shock as I kept asking, "How did this happen to me?"

For months I wallowed in shame, fear, anger, and frustration. My weekly job hunt only resulted in rejection after rejection, and with each rejection, my sense of shame and worthlessness grew. I frequently thought, "I should go back to my volunteer work at the mission since I have lots of time on my hands," but I couldn't quite do it.

How in the world could I face anybody, much less a homeless crowd, and bring messages of hope when I too worried that I would default on my bills, lose my home, and end up homeless? I couldn't inspire hope because I was utterly hopeless.

Restless nights turned into tearful seasons of hibernation and extreme desperation until I finally hit rock bottom. I cried out, "Dear God, I don't know what to do!", and He whispered back to me, "Then DO what I've called you to DO. You've always had a job. Take Mark 16:15 to heart and go and share the Gospel."

He [Jesus] said to them, "Go into all the world and preach the gospel to all creation." (Mark 16:15 NIV)

Reality hit hard as I realized God had just offered me a job—a job that came with no pay but incredible benefits. My job was to go back to the very place where I feared I would face the most embarrassment (the shelter) and share the Gospel message with a renewed, but nonetheless brutal, honesty about God's love for me in a season of brokenness. So, I finally placed that call to the mission and said, "I'm back in service!"

A few weeks later, with Bible, sweet snacks, and sticky notes in hand, I showed up at the women's shelter, trembling like a leaf. How would these ladies respond to the raw truths God has been teaching me? How could I inspire them to trust when I stood there not knowing how I would pay this month's mortgage? How could I tell these ladies to love Jesus when I believed He had abandoned me? I felt anything but prepared to go to the shelter, but still, I went. I got up, showed up, and did something. And consequently, He did something that took my breath away.

During the week of Easter, I returned to the shelter, as God had gently placed the word "shame" on my restless heart. I painfully dug into my fifteen months of unemployment shame, using real-world pain to remind the ladies that they faced no shame in the shadow of the cross.

That night the ladies, children, and I laughed, cried, hugged, and prayed in powerful ways. It was one of the most beautiful Easter celebrations I've ever been a part of. God used my crisis of shame to share the hope of salvation. He honored my willingness to show up and "do something" with the Gospel, even though I wasn't sure what I was doing.

Have you ever experienced a similar season of frustration, doubt, or shame? Have you perhaps felt like God cannot use you because you're too broken? If so, you're not alone. Maybe, in recent months, you've thought about signing up to help with the singles, senior adult, or preschool ministries at church, or you've weighed a decision to serve meals at a homeless shelter, but your fear has kept you away.

Maybe you're the woman or man dealing with a struggling marriage, a wayward teenager, physical pain, or the rejection of a lost love, and you just don't feel put together enough to serve or do anything, much less "volunteer" to be a ministry helper. If that's where you've been or are, then I have good news for you! It's OK.

Even God's most devoted believers have felt doubt. But the Bible reminds us that God's call to do something in the Kingdom never requires us to be "fixed." Instead, His call on our lives often works best in our brokenness.

Let's consider: The majority of God's calls for service, as reflected in the Scripture, begin with direct verbs: "Go, Do, Show, Seek," for example. And they avoid any mention of our frequently uttered disclaimers, disclaimers that often start with, "I'll serve when …"

Mark 16:15 is one of the Bible's greatest examples of God's direct call to jump in and do something. When God says, "Go and share," He refuses to add, "When you feel up to it."

In short, when God calls upon us to show up, speak up, and do something, we don't have the luxury of putting His call on hold. His call for us is to be ready to go and tell others about Jesus' saving grace, even when it's the last thing we want to do.

If we think about the way that Jesus called His disciples, He didn't give them time to reflect. His call to the first four disciples, Peter, Andrew, James, and John, was direct: "Come, follow me" (Matthew 4:19 NIV). And they came, messy lives included. In similar fashion, God's call on each of our lives today is to come as we are and report for duty.

If this season of life finds you hurting, weeping, feeling discouraged, or utterly broken from life's greatest hardships, remember this: you're in the best spot for God to call and use you to do great things. God does His most powerful work through our brokenness, and if you don't believe me, then put Him to the test.

If you're scared to engage, just go ahead and sign up, show up, and do something at the place He calls you to serve, whether it's the local laundry mat, baseball field, or church sanctuary. You'll be amazed at how rapidly He turns your message of brokenness into a testimony of beauty.

Prayer:

Dear God, Help me remember You've not called me to perfection, but rather to purpose. Your call on my life asks me to be willing to get up, sign up, and show up. I may not know how, where, or why You want to use me, and we both know I don't feel ready to serve, but nonetheless, I'm showing up. Help me exercise a little faith and get excited about how, where, and why You have chosen me to pour truth into hurting people today. I will trust You in this season and do something with abandon.

Questions:

1. Why do you think doing service or missions work is scary to many believers?

2. Can you think of a life experience that left you with a powerful testimony of God's greater purpose for service?

3. If God is willing to use us in our moments of pain and hardship, what does that tell us about His love for us?

Weakness: The Devastating Impact of Doing Nothing
by Ron Gallagher

I have arrived at a point in life where I am blessed to have acquired several fake body parts. Well, I suppose I shouldn't call them "fake," since that makes them sound like they're a collection of second class knockoffs sold alongside those imitation Rolex® watches sold by street vendors in New York. My new body parts are actually the genuine article, and though I didn't think to ask, maybe they even have designer labels on them. My joints might even be the same kind that are sought after by all the "A List" celebrities and social icons. Regardless, they are not original equipment. While I'm overwhelmed with gratitude to God for my artificial joints, replacement eye lenses, and various other gadgets here and there, I've learned a few things through the process that I would have been happy not to know.

A Learning Process Begins ~

For instance, a total of three joint replacement surgeries over an eight-month period of time recently taught me that creating weakness is easy. It's one of the few things left in this culture that we can do without pulling up a "how-to" video on YouTube. The procedure is really quite simple. If we stop doing things that promote and maintain strength, weakness will develop on its own. For months, physical limitation became a lifestyle, causing muscle groups that weren't even directly involved in the surgical process to be adversely affected, and weakness began to spread. Simply said, the less I did, the less I was able to do, and the less I was able to do, the less I wanted to do.

Weakness is obviously debilitating even in regard to simple, routine tasks, but there are other potential repercussions. Physical weakness can eventually affect immune systems, and that can provide an open door invitation to the invasion of all kinds of other diseases and disorders, increasing negative influences to mental and emotional responses as well. Weakness can alter desire, sabotage self-confidence, and undermine one's sense of value. No wonder God repeatedly admonished His people to "Be strong."

> *Watch, stand fast in the faith, be brave, be strong.* (1 Corinthians 16:13 NKJV')
> *Finally, my brethren, be strong in the Lord and in the power of His might.* (Ephesians 6:10)
> *You therefore, my son, be strong in the grace that is in Christ Jesus.* (2 Timothy 2:1)

The simple truth is that the impact of inactivity and weakness in a human body is also true of the Church. When the Body of Christ ceases to perform those tasks it was designed, equipped, and commissioned to do, weakness will result, and if it persists, inability will follow and eventually even the desire to do those things will erode. When spiritual weakness consumes a church, all kinds of destructive philosophies and perverse doctrines will make opportunistic inroads. Weakness can reduce a church to a powerless, pathetic parody of what it was designed to be.

Action Is Mandatory ~

Creating weakness is always easy, but regaining lost strength is hard. God's call to "be strong" can never be accomplished passively. Weakened legs never become strong again by sitting in a recliner wishing for it. The dangerous product of doing nothing cannot be defeated unless it is challenged and overcome by actively doing something. Dormant body parts have to be pushed past their comfortable boundaries in spite of their painful protests. Tasks and activities cannot be allowed the luxury of waiting until some wave of motivational inspiration comes along. Purpose must overcome pleasure.

Becoming weak is easy for the church as well. It happens when we stop doing what we were designed, equipped, and commissioned to do. In America, it seems as though somewhere along the line, the cultural impact of Jesus' mandate to teach them *to observe all things that I have commanded you* (Matthew 28:20), has grown weaker and weaker. Instead of teaching followers of Jesus to "observe," that is, "do," all those things He commanded us to do, it seems that a growing number of churches have reinterpreted His words in the "Great Commission." It seems instead to have become, "Entice as many people as possible to come to your meeting center and enjoy the praise and worship while being careful not to quote anything from the Bible that could be potentially offensive."

Good News ~

Regaining strength in either a physical or spiritual context will always be difficult, but the good news is that it can be done. The other good news is that the admonition to be strong does not demand something from us that we do not have. It's a call to action, but it doesn't require us to do things we cannot do. Regaining strength physically begins as simply as getting out of the recliner. Then it requires investing the strength we have in whatever increments we can muster toward doing things in accordance with God's design.

A few months ago, following one of my surgeries, I attempted to take a walk in our neighborhood. It's familiar territory, and not so long ago, my prayer walks would sometimes go up to five miles at a time. On that occasion, though, I barely made it half a block before I was worn out and had to stop. It was embarrassing, and I was disturbed at how weak I had become and how hard it was to do such a simple thing. I had to give up for that day, but there were other days that would follow. I have kept taking those walks as often as I can, and though some days are harder than others, giving up was not an option. Last week I decided to take another prayer walk, and it turned out to be about three and a half miles.

Doing things, even little things, has power we don't always recognize in the moment. Fulfilling God's desire that we be strong may sometimes be demonstrated by explosive individual effort, but those are the exceptions. The most powerful examples of enduring strength appear when we faithfully begin to string together a pattern of doing the little things that we can do. Remember, a tiny rock made a giant fall, so dream small.[1]

Prayer:

Father, Help us to be spiritually strong. Lead us daily so that weakness claims no hold over any part of our lives. Let us not drift into it, become paralyzed with it because of inactivity or carelessness, or persist in the habits of life that inevitably produce it. Help us to be faithful in doing those little things that produce greater spiritual strength. Lead us past spending our time on wasteful or empty activities to tending to Your good purposes. In Jesus' name, Amen.

Questions:

1. What are some areas of life in which you would like to be stronger, and what "exercises" might help you attain it?

2. Which "little things" would help most of us to be stronger spiritually?

3. In 1 Corinthians 16:13, how do the four commands complement each other? Why are they all needed, and particularly, what contribution does "be strong" make?

---

*All Scripture verses are taken from the NKJV.
1. Based on "Dream Small," a song by Josh Wilson.

Share the Love
by Katherine Pasour

My hands pulled weeds automatically, my mind far away from the mundane task. The rich aroma of freshly delivered mulch normally soothed me, but today I was wound as tight as the spool of cord on my weed-eater. I removed the last of the weeds and gathered the discarded clump to add to the compost pile behind the house. I pondered the dead leaves and wilted stems, a stark reminder of my broken life.

What are you going to do?

"Excuse me."

I straightened from my task of spreading mulch on the freshly weeded bed of hostas. Since moving to the neighborhood two months before, I'd noticed my neighbor from across the street, but we hadn't yet met.

"Hello." I tried to sound friendly.

She smiled—a big smile with lots of teeth. I'd never seen such a joyous smile. We traded introductions, and she complimented my yard. Her outgoing personality surrounded me, penetrating my introvert shield of protection with darts of enthusiasm and exuberance. I wanted to retreat, anxious to avoid her "real" reason for visiting.

"I'm starting a Bible study and wanted to invite you."

What?

"A Bible study?" I stammered.

I'd never felt so far away from God as I had in these two months of separation from my husband.

You need to do this. I heard the voice in my head as my neighbor waited for my response. I opened my mouth to decline—to verbalize some excuse. But the speaker in my head persisted as my neighbor rambled on.

"I know you work during the week, but the study will be on Saturday mornings. Will that be convenient for you?"

Again, I prepared words to express my gratitude, while offering an excuse. But the answer that came from my mouth was, "Yes, Saturday mornings are convenient."

Once more, that wide grin set her face aglow. "That's wonderful! We start a week from Saturday."

My thoughts swirled as I watched her walk back across the street.

What have I done?

Last night I had succumbed to doubt and fear, flinging myself across the bed as I cried out to God to help me pull myself from the depths of despair.

> *Search me, God, and know my heart;*
> *test me and know my anxious thoughts.*
> *See if there is any offensive way in me,*
> *and lead me in the way everlasting.*
> (Psalm 139:23-24 NIV)

I scoffed as I cried out to God for help. Of course He will find me offensive. Hadn't I left my husband? Separated him from his daughter? How could that not be offensive?

Will God forgive me? Can my husband forgive me? How can I get out of this pit of sin?

The quest for control pulled me into the pit. I turned away from God, ignoring Him. I chose disobedience and willfully stepped onto the path of sin.

I couldn't get out of the pit on my own power.

But God had another plan. He chose a Christian neighbor and sent her to me in my time of need. This stranger, who became a beloved friend, listened to God's call and accepted the challenge to intervene in my life.

Then I heard the voice of the Lord saying, "Whom shall I send? And who will go for us?"
And I said, "Here am I. Send me!" (Isaiah 6:8)

God saw my need and heard my plea for help. He asked my neighbor, "Whom shall I send to help her?"

My neighbor answered, "Here I am, Lord, send me."

Even though she was not aware of my particular need, she answered God's call anyway. She didn't hesitate to approach a stranger and offer love and the message of redemption. My neighbor didn't know me, but she understood God's request to intervene in my life. My heavenly Father nudged my neighbor to reach a hand to rescue me from the pit of sin. She didn't hesitate.

He lifted me out of the slimy pit, out of the mud and mire;
he set my feet on a rock and gave me a firm place to stand.
He put a new song in my mouth, a hymn of praise to our God.
(Psalm 40:2-3)

The Bible study was a life-changing experience for me. My neighbor and the other amazing women in that study loved me, prayed for me, and encouraged my baby steps on this new journey. God sent His amazing love pulsing through them and guided their actions to support me in the path of repentance and redemption.

Sometimes it's terrifying for us to step out into the unknown. Although it's obvious that my neighbor and friend is an extrovert and comfortable speaking in almost any situation, she later confessed that approaching me that memorable day made her nervous. But, she didn't question God's call to action. She acted in response to God's directive to reach out to me, even before she knew my situation. My neighbor put her own apprehension aside, stepped across the street into unchartered territory, and put witness into action.

Can we?

Prayer:

In Your infinite wisdom, Father, You always seem to know when to send a helper into our lives. "Thank you" seems such an inadequate response for the love, peace, grace, and mercy You bestow upon us, and we are so grateful. Without Your guidance, we would be lost. We would be mired in a pit of sin. But You listen to our cries for help. You surround us with Your love, and You send those special people into our lives just when needed. Thank You for giving us the strength and courage to *do* in service to You. In the precious name of Jesus, Amen.

Questions:

1. Read Matthew 25:31-46. My neighbor acted—she "did for the least of these"—when she responded to God's call to intervene in my sinful life.

   Is God calling you to action? Is there a need—someone hungry, in need of shelter, or in a prison of hurt and despair that you need to reach out to? What can you "do for the least of these"?

2. The prophet Isaiah responded to God's call by saying, *"Here am I. Send me."* Have you felt the nudging (or call) from God to complete a specific task in service to Him? Did you answer the call? What was that experience like for you? Has there been

a time when God called you and you did not answer? What happened then? How did you feel?

3. When you feel God calling you to a specific action, how do you proceed? Do you make an action plan? Do you share your plan with a friend and ask him or her to prayerfully provide you with feedback or suggestions?

4. Read Romans 7:14-25. Paul reminds us of the struggle to *do* good. He affirms that evil is by our side, tirelessly seeking to engage our sinful nature.

   Sometimes when we feel called to *do*, this action may be instigated by evil. What strategies have worked for you to discern being called to do good according to God's will, or being urged toward evil by our sinful nature?

---

*All Scripture verses are taken from the NIV.

The Power of Consistency
by Barbara Latta

And whatever you do, do it heartily,
as to the Lord and not to men,
knowing that from the Lord you will receive
the reward of the inheritance;
for you serve the Lord Christ.
(Colossians 3:23-24 NKJV)

After staring at my computer screen for what seemed like hours, I turned the machine off leaving the blinking cursor on the blank page. Frustration at my writing endeavors plagued me along with other areas of my life. Bible reading was sporadic, and exercise nonexistent. I couldn't figure out why I had a dissatisfaction in my soul.

Reading success stories of other people was supposed to inspire me to follow in their footsteps. Instead I fell into the hole of comparison, and my mind attacked me with words of condemnation for all the things I had let go by in years past.

I had been asking God what was wrong, but along with my hit-and-miss Bible reading, my listening wasn't on track either. One day while reading in Hebrews about laboring to rest, I meditated on that lesson and thought more deeply about God's rest. Resting means listening, absorbing, and turning off everything but God's Word.

When I rested, I could hear. And what I heard in my spirit was, *Consistency is the key.*

Consistency is the key? What does that mean, Lord?

Then I remembered that I had been asking Him why my life was filled with so much frustration. It was because I wasn't disciplined and consistent in anything I was doing. My writing was in bits and pieces, not in a scheduled time like I hear all the successful writing teachers say we should do. Bible reading was when I had time in the morning, or a quick devotion at lunch, and the exercise, well, let's just say the treadmill makes a good storage rack.

Consistency and diligence can be twin characteristics. According to the dictionary, *consistency* is "harmony or conduct of practice with profession"[1] and the word *diligence* is defined as "steady, earnest and energetic effort: persevering application."[2]

My loving heavenly Father was telling me that achievement depended on steadfastness in whatever goal is being pursued. Consistency in writing will complete a book, in Bible study will bring enlightenment, and in exercise will strengthen muscles.

My resolve that day was to start getting up earlier in the mornings to read the Bible in the quietness of the day. I started a regular writing schedule, and the dust was blown off the treadmill. The first few steps were somewhat squeaky after the machine had experienced months of no use.

Paul lived a life of consistent discipline. Even when he was terrorizing Christians, he never wavered from his goal. His misplaced passion pushed him toward what he thought was a defense of God. After encountering Christ, that same passion was now guided in the right direction. When he was persecuted, he didn't give in. He didn't forget the task God had laid upon his shoulders, and the world at that time was turned upside down because of his influence. Diligence in his work caused him to write most of the New Testament, and his words are still impacting us today.

He wrote from prison. Chains and bonds didn't stop him. He continued to travel. Shipwrecks and storms didn't stop him. He was told to keep quiet. Threats didn't stop him.

He pushed through the hardships of life and pressed toward the prize of the high calling of Christ (Philippians 3:14).

We are all given a high calling from Christ. We may not be Pauls and Peters, but we do have a sphere of influence. What we do in our personal lives will spill over into our relationships. Constant faithfulness in following Christ and His Words will determine how powerful that impression will be.

The most consistent person who ever lived was Jesus. We have no better example of life and discipline. When people were pulling Him in every direction, He still took the time to spend with His Father because it was the most important thing in His life—even when it meant losing sleep and praying all night (Luke 6:12).

If consistency and diligence reign, it's easier to put priorities in order. When Christ is the most important person in our lives, we can hear what He is saying. Consistency drowns out distractions, strengthens resolve against attacks, and builds new habits that can last a lifetime.

My decision to pursue a more focused lifestyle brought some rewards. I wrote and self-published my first book. Holding that printed form and caressing the cover brought great satisfaction. I knew I had not done this on my own. Without God, I could not have finished a book, but His patience and push to write every day produced a result. I have filled notebooks and journals with the insight the Lord has given me because of the decision to get out of bed an hour earlier in the morning. The treadmill is in my writing office, and when sitting too long wears on me, I know walking is what my legs need.

The power of consistency has shown me the key to success, and a rewarded life has been my prize.

Prayer:

Heavenly Father, Thank You for being the consistent God that You are. You never waver, and Your Word shows me how to stand on Your promises to make my life complete. Amen.

Questions:

1. What does Proverbs 21:5 tell us will be the reward of a diligent life?

2. According to 1 Timothy 4:15-16, why should we pay close attention to what we are teaching to others through our life and words?

3. What does 2 Peter 1:10 tell us we can do to make sure we never stumble? (Also see v.5-7.)

4. According to Hebrews 6:12, whom should we imitate?

---

1. Merriam-Webster Online, s. v. "consistency," https://www.merriam-webster.com/dictionary/consistency.
2. Ibid., s. v. "diligence," https://www.merriamwebster.com/dictionary/diligence.

Be Anxious for Nothing
by Dorcas Asercion Zuniga

Anxious.

That's how I felt after I finished taking the recertification test for the American Board of Family Medicine. It had been ten years since I recertified. Getting in my studying had been harder this time, so I didn't feel as prepared.

The Board would notify each test taker within a week, by email, if we passed or if our score was "pending further review." The pass or fail for the latter group depended on the scores of all who sat for the Boards throughout the several weeks of that session.

As I had feared, I received the "pending further review" email. Now I had to wait for two months to receive the final verdict. Two long months.

"Be anxious for nothing." Those words swirled in my mind, but I couldn't stop worrying.

> *Do not be anxious about anything, but in every situation, by prayer and petition, with thanksgiving, present your requests to* [Yahweh*]. *And the peace of* [Yahweh], *which transcends all understanding, will guard your hearts and your minds in* [Messiah Yeshua*]. (Philippians 4:6-7 NIV)

In the New King James Version, Philippians 4:6 starts with "Be anxious for nothing." What was there to be anxious about?

Nothing. If I failed, I could still practice. And I could always retest. So, why did I worry?

There was a time, years before, when the result of a test was not in my favor. It was early in my pregnancy, and my screening test for potential birth defects came back positive.

My obstetrician tried to reassure me that my baby had a statistically greater chance of being healthy. But I was an older mother-to-be. I knew my risk was higher to give birth to a child with special needs.

There was something else that I also knew. I knew that having this baby was Yahweh's will. After two unsuccessful attempts at in vitro fertilization, this was my "miracle baby." My husband and I thanked our Heavenly Father for this marvelous gift He would soon place into our waiting arms. And that peace that Paul promised to the Philippians filled and guarded my heart. I rested in the knowledge that our son would be born the way he was meant to be—fashioned by the very Hands of the Master of all creation.

So why was I so anxious about the results of my recertification test when I was at such peace over the health of my son? It was because I was uncertain of the will of Yahweh for my career.

In every situation, by prayer and petition, with thanksgiving, present your requests to [Yahweh].

Eventually, I changed my request. I asked Yahweh that His will be done and thanked Him for doing what was best for me.

And His peace filled and guarded my heart and mind.

Wouldn't it be nice to skip the worry and go straight to the peace? I recently received the devasting news that one of my dear patients had breast cancer. When I spoke with her, she told me, "I'm at peace." Here I was, worrying about her and her lovely family. Because she had placed her life in Yahweh's Hands long ago, she was not anxious about anything. Such faith!

Worry, even over the smallest thing, can overtake us and strip us of our joy. Thankfully, there are promises in the Bible that encourage us when we are the most vulnerable.

You will keep him in perfect peace, whose mind is stayed on You, because he trusts in You. (Isaiah 26:3 NKJV)

Cast all your anxiety on him because he cares for you. (1 Peter 5:7 NIV)

But seek first his kingdom and his righteousness, and all these things will be given to you as well. Therefore do not worry about tomorrow, for tomorrow will worry about itself. (Matthew 6:33-34 NIV)

I know the plans I have in mind for you—it is Yahweh who speaks—plans for peace, not disaster, reserving a future full of hope for you. (Jeremiah 29:11 TJB**)

And we know that in all things [Yahweh] *works for the good of those who love him, who have been called according to his purpose.* (Romans 8:28 NIV)

These are just some of the verses that resonate through my heart and mind when I am anxious. The Spirit used these words to see me through my pregnancy and, years later, the waiting period for my test score. Yahweh saw fit to give me a healthy son and a favorable outcome for my Boards. But even if His answers were different, I knew I could continue onward because He guarded my heart with His peace.

"Be anxious for nothing." Our future, our very lives are safe in the Hands of the One who created the universe. He cares for us and takes care of our tomorrows. He has reserved a future of hope for each one of us. We can rest assured that He works all things for our good.

And when we present our requests to Him, with thanksgiving in our hearts, He will give us a peace that transcends all understanding.

Prayer:

Dear Father in Heaven, Thank You for guarding my heart and mind with Your peace when I bring my requests to You. Help me to remember that I don't have to be anxious because my life is in Your Hands.

Questions:

1. What situation are you the most worried about? How are you coping with it?

2. What Bible promise helps you when you are anxious?

3. How does being thankful help you gain peace even in times of difficulty?

---

*Author's Note: Yahweh is the revealed Hebrew name of God the Father, and Yeshua is the Hebrew name of Jesus, our Messiah and risen Savior. Thank you for letting me share these special names with you.

**Alexander Jones, General Editor, *The Jerusalem Bible Reader's Edition*, (Garden City, New York: Doubleday & Company, Inc., 1966).

Let Go of Dangerous Things
by Jenifer Kitchens

My ten-year-old daughter is very protective of her baby brother, and at nine months old, he is getting into everything. Not too long ago, she stepped away from her homework and the little guy seized the opportunity to get his hands on her pencil. He was quite pleased with himself, but we knew the danger. We didn't want him to harm himself with the sharp point.

We responded quickly. We gently pried his fingers open so that he would let go of the pencil and offered him a toy that was more age appropriate. He eagerly reached for the ball that jingled.

My son isn't the only one who tries to hold onto things that aren't good for him—things that are even dangerous for him. I do this, too. Usually, it's not my fingers but my heart that is clinging so tightly to dangerous ideas or emotions.

In Ephesians, Paul gives instructions on how we should walk as Christians. In the middle of these instructions, Chapter 4, verse 31 (NASB) says, "Let all bitterness and wrath and anger and clamor and slander be put away from you, along with all malice."

Paul gives us a specific directive to let things be put away from us—things that will hinder our relationship with Christ and the world around us, things that can hold our heart and mind captive. If we want them to be put away from us, that means we have to let go of them. We can't hang on. It also means that getting rid of them isn't something we do on our own. God alone is the one who removes them from us after we let go.

My little guy had a grip on something that could potentially be devastating to him. Just as we had to get him to let go of it so that we could remove it from him, God wants us to let go so He can remove from us things that will devastate our hearts.

What things do we need to let go of? Bitterness, wrath, anger, clamor, slander, and malice. When we or someone we love has been wronged (or we think so and we really don't see the situation correctly), it's so easy to want to hang on to bitterness, wrath, and anger. These emotions cloud our thinking, though. Our heart, the source of our emotions, lies to us (Jeremiah 17:9). It tells us we have a right to these emotions when we really don't.

I really struggle with letting go of clamor so that it can be put away from me. Clamor is confusing noise, different voices shouting at us. We hear the clamor of our culture fighting for our attention, but there can also be clamor that comes from rehearsing negative self-talk and repeating back to ourselves the lies that have been spoken over us. Too often I realize that I am defending myself to accusations and jeers that no one hears but me. We need to let go of both of these kinds of clamor, internal and external, so that God can remove it from us.

Slander and malice are pervasive in the world around us. Turn on any political news show, or even the late night television, and the goal seems to be to make someone else look bad—and if the truth won't do it, it can be "bent" just a bit to accomplish the goal. Misrepresenting someone with the intent of changing someone's opinion of them is wrong; it has no place in our lives. As Christians, we have no business participating in slander or malice. We must let it be put away from us as we become more like Christ.

We must also let go of slanderous words spoken and malicious actions taken against us. Paul saw the ills of both participating in and harboring the effects of this sin; he refers to both sides in the next verse. "Be kind to one another, tender-hearted, forgiving each other, just as God in Christ also has forgiven you" (Ephesians 4:32 NASB). He set Christ as the standard. We should act like Christ, and we should forgive like Christ. We need to let go of things that hinder this so God can put them away from us.

In picking up that sharp pencil, my son was only doing what came naturally to him. His natural actions, though, resulted in a potentially dangerous situation, and that pencil needed to be put away from him. Bitterness, wrath, anger, clamor, slander, and malice are natural responses, but are damaging. We need to let go of them so our Loving Father can remove them from us.

Prayer:

Creator God who made me with the capacity to both feel and act, please forgive me when my feelings reign in my heart and mind instead of You. I confess that my actions don't always reflect Your love and compassion. Please help me to let go of the emotions and actions that keep me from looking like You, that hinder my spiritual journey, and that place a stumbling block in front of those that don't have a relationship with You. I trust that You want good things for me. Thank You for loving me and giving me Jesus as a model for my life.

Questions:

1. Of bitterness, wrath, anger, clamor, slander, and malice, which of these do you struggle with the most?

2. Why do you think this particular issue has this kind of place in your heart and mind?

3. How would your family be different if you collectively let go of these?

4. How would letting go of these, change your church?

5. It's one thing to be kind to someone. You can put on a facade and do this for a while. Why is it important that we also are tenderhearted and forgive as Christ forgave?

Driven by Compassion
by Brad Simon

It was early in the morning and the sun was just about to creep above the horizon. In a few hours the scorching sun would be beating down on the dry desert land. Even though it was early in the morning, sleep began to fill his eyes as he wearily prepared for his travels.

He had just spent the past twenty-four hours teaching the multitudes, and now he had a day's journey ahead of him. He had already sent the rest of his traveling companions around the peninsula by boat in the cool Mediterranean breeze. Rather than spending the day below deck being gently swayed to sleep by the waves of the sea, he would travel by foot on the dusty, rocky trail over the mountain and join them on the other side.

He would not make the journey alone. The men who would go with him were the reason for the journey. This would be the last time he would ever see them, and he just had to spend those few precious hours together that day. He would not sleep the day away when there was work yet to be done. He could not! The Apostle Paul was driven by his purpose, and he had a message he needed to impart to the Christians in Troas.

Why was Paul so committed to working night and day? I believe the answer is found in his letter to the Corinthians. He said, *"Be imitators of me, as I am of Christ?"* (1 Corinthians 11:1 ESV).

In his gospel, Matthew revealed Jesus' driving motivation and what He wants us to do today.

> *And Jesus went throughout all the cities and villages, teaching in their synagogues and proclaiming the gospel of the kingdom and healing every disease and every affliction. When he saw the crowds, he had compassion for them, because they were harassed and helpless, like sheep without a shepherd. Then he said to his disciples, "The harvest is plentiful, but the laborers are few; therefore pray earnestly to the Lord of the harvest to send out laborers into his harvest."* (Matthew 9:35-38 ESV)

There are four characteristics of Jesus in this passage that we, like Paul, are to imitate.

1. **First, Jesus saw the crowds**. To have a ministry like Paul, we need to see people as Jesus saw them. We need to stop and look and see them the way they are—hurting, lost, and confused, like sheep without a shepherd. How often do we meet people today and ask them how they are doing? We hear what they say, but do we really listen? Do we see their difficulties, their troubles, and their concerns? Just like Elisha prayed that God would open his servant's eyes to see the army of the Lord, we need to pray that God will open our eyes to see as Jesus saw.

2. **Next, we need to feel as Jesus felt**. Unlike the Pharisees, He did not see their lowly state and take pride in the fact that He was not like them. Jesus put Himself in their shoes. He felt their pain. He felt their heartaches. He had compassion for them. He did not just feel sorry for them; He had empathy for them. He hurt along with their hurts. When we see people as Jesus saw them, the Holy Spirit will work within us to begin feeling the way Jesus felt. He will move us to have compassion on them.

3. **Then we need to pray like Jesus prayed**. Jesus told the disciples to pray earnestly to the Lord. He prayed for the people and for the Father to send workers to meet their needs. How often do we tell people we will pray for them, but in reality we forget about them? And when we do remember to pray, do we

pray powerful, effective prayers? A weak prayer life leads to a weak ministry.

4. **Finally, we need to do as Jesus did**. His compassion moved Him to action. He got involved with the people. He reached out and met the needs of those around him. He prayed for God the Father to send workers and then was willing Himself to be the worker sent. Like the prophet Isaiah who prayed, "Here am I! Send me" (Isaiah 6:8 ESV). We need to be willing to get involved in our prayers, engaged in the lives of the people we see around us.

Like Jesus, Paul had a compassion for people. He saw the new Christians in the churches he started and knew they needed to be discipled to maturity in Christ. He saw the people in the towns he traveled to and saw the aimless lives they led, and he had to tell them about the saving grace of Jesus Christ. He had such a compassion for people he had no choice. As he did in Troas in Acts Chapter 20, he had to work night and day, often without sleep, to accomplish his ministry.

Are you ready to imitate Paul, just as he imitated Christ? Are you willing to see as Jesus saw, feel as Jesus felt, pray as Jesus prayed, and do as Jesus did? Those are the characteristics for a compassionate, powerful ministry that any Christian can have, and one that God wants us to have. A ministry that will make a difference in the lives of people.

Prayer:

Father, Help us to see people and value them, to empathize with their cares and concerns, to be faithful in prayer for others, and to do what You direct us to do to help. Help us to know what part we have in Your gracious plan to reach people with the gospel of Christ and to bless them with a growing knowledge of Your word. Lead us and coach us in imitating Christ in His compassion that makes such a welcome difference in our lives. In Jesus' name, Amen.

Questions:

1. Is there any part of ministry to the church or to the lost that you are drawn to?

2. Why do you want to participate in that ministry?

3. Which of the four ways in this study that we can imitate Christ, resonates with you?

4. What insights about Jesus do these four ways give you?

5. How does compassion overcome some of the hindrances and challenges to a continuing ministry? Which Bible verses may help us with that?

Learning to Cling
by Lisa Kibler

The waves lashed the thirty-five foot sailboat, and I dithered between clinging to my husband, Sam, and thrusting my head over the edge of the vessel. The fate of my lunch was undecided. "Will I digest it, or will it cause this body to heave like Lake Erie's water?"

The boat was leaning. Leaning way too much for me, a first-time sailor (and most likely, last). In wonder, I watched Sam's boss balance on the boom of the mainsail and then fall easily back as if onto a hammock. His vessel, his comfort zone.

What on earth? I wish I had his chutzpah and confidence.

He cut a commanding figure on the boom. And I wished one day to garner the fearlessness to cling so, to that which I loved.

The disciple Peter loved Jesus, but he had to learn to cling to Him.

Once Jesus asked His disciples to go across the Sea of Galilee to the "other side" while He spent time alone to pray (Matthew 14:22-33). While the disciples were rowing far from shore, the wind and waves rocked their boat. Jesus, ruler of the heavens and the earth, walked on the water to them. When they saw Him, they "cried out in fear" (v.26 ESV*), thinking Him a ghost. Jesus said, "Take heart; it is I. Do not be afraid" (v.27).

Bolstered by his Lord, Peter asked Jesus to command that he go to Him on the water—a demonstration of his faith. Jesus said, "Come" (v.29), and we all know what Peter did. He started in faith, and then he took his eyes off Jesus and began to sink, crying out to Jesus, "Lord, save me!" (v.30). Jesus, full of love and compassion (and a rebuke of Peter's weak faith), pulled him up, and both of them got into the boat and the wind ceased. Those in the boat worshiped Jesus and said, "Truly you are the Son of God" (v.33).

Peter would face another test of faith.

Within a few short years, Jesus, focused on the reason He came, faced His betrayer in the Garden of Gethsemane. He stood before Caiaphas, the high priest, and acknowledged that indeed He is the Christ, the Son of God. But Peter, the disciple who had claimed the same truth about Christ at Caesarea Philippi, hid his allegiance—three times—just as Jesus declared to him earlier that night that he would. And when the rooster crowed, "Peter remembered the saying of Jesus, 'Before the rooster crows, you will deny me three times.' And he went out and wept bitterly" (Matthew 26:75).

After his death, burial, and resurrection, Jesus appeared to the disciples as they hid out of fear of the Jews. Three times, three times in John 20, Jesus said, "Peace be with you" (v.19, 21, 26).

Jesus revealed Himself to the disciples a second time (this time as they were behind locked doors), and then again. Soon after the emotional milieu of the previous days, Peter decided to go fishing along with six other disciples (John 21:1-14). He sought to escape back to his previous life, a life where he could simply throw out a net and try not to remember his failure—denying Jesus. The man whom Jesus said would be a fisher of men, thought his sin had disqualified him from obeying his calling. He loved Jesus, and yet may have doubted that he loved Him enough.

While the disciples were in their boat waiting for the fish, they saw Jesus standing on the shore. When John realized it was Jesus, Peter, without hesitation "put on his outer garment … and threw himself into the sea" (v.7). Peter went from a doubting disciple (Matthew 14) to one who forgot fear to get to his Lord.

Only twice in Scripture is a charcoal fire mentioned. The first one warmed Peter before he denied Christ three times. The second one Jesus made to grill some of the disciples' catch of fish (John 21:9). Why would Jesus make a charcoal fire? Our sense of smell is strong, and certain aromas evoke memories. Perhaps Jesus stirred Peter's memory of his failure.

Jesus said, "Simon, son of John, do you love me more than these?" (v.15). Jesus called him Simon because Peter had gone back to his previous life. Did Peter love Jesus? Why did Jesus ask Peter if he loved Him?

In John's gospel, the word Jesus used most often for love, is *agapaō* (or *agape*). In this sense, it means a willful love, a fondness and a desire for what is best for another. In John 21:15 and 17, Jesus used this word when He asked Peter if he loved Him. Peter had outwardly demonstrated his love for Christ when he threw himself in the sea to get to Jesus, and when he hauled the net full of fish ashore as the Master directed. Peter's passion for Jesus was no secret.

In verse 17, though, Peter used the word, *phileō*, to answer Jesus' question. The word refers to friendship and relational intimacy (as dear friends). Jesus asked Peter if he loved Him to get Peter to acknowledge it. Three times Peter told Jesus that he loved Him, just as three times he had denied Jesus on the night of His betrayal. Jesus wanted Peter to know that he was forgiven, and their relationship was intact. Peter was fully restored. He was prepared for the work that he would do for Christ on and after Pentecost.

What does clinging to Jesus look like for us?

Peter feared that his past sin would deny him the ability and opportunity to serve Jesus, to do what he was called to do. But Jesus taught Peter, and us, that our sins do not define us. Who we were before, is not who we are now. We need to know this, or guilt and shame will propel us backward. Jesus exposed Peter's sin and restored him. Every time our sin is exposed, we get the chance to make a "gospel reply," such as "I believe the gospel. I proclaim it, and I know the power of cancelled sin is removed." We know that all of our mistakes can be used by God for our benefit. His redemption draws us forward and allows us to serve Jesus with full vigor. It's in Him that we find our worth and our value. We do what He has called us to do, for our good and His glory.

I didn't go sailing again, but I have a confidence in Christ that I lacked when I watched Sam's boss on that mainsail boom. Now I can confidently lean in to Jesus as I serve Him, knowing He will never let me fall.

Prayer:

Most gracious heavenly Father, Thank You for the many ways You teach us by how You taught Jesus' disciples. You waste nothing, and we love, trust, and believe with great expectancy, knowing You never slumber. Help us as we seek Your will in our lives, and when we falter or doubt how we can be used, remind us of Peter and Jesus' gentle and complete restoration of him. May we do with great joy that which You have called us to do. No doubts. No fear. Just humble and open hearts. In the matchless name of Jesus, Amen.

Questions:

1. Has Jesus ever restored you from an instance or season of weak faith?

2. Where you are now in your walk with Christ, are you more likely to "do" doubt or faith?

3. What has the Lord called you to do?

4. What steps will you take to maintain your focus on serving Jesus in all you do?

---

*All Scripture verses are taken from the ESV.

The Risk of Obedience
by Mary Holloman

Their steady paces and lighthearted banter masked their racing hearts. The two girls scanned the faces they passed on their college campus: a guy wearing headphones, a girl talking on the phone, a couple holding hands. Up ahead, the girls saw a cluster of benches where a student sat alone, scrolling on her phone. The girls glanced at each other, nodded in silent agreement, and headed straight for the benches.

"Excuse me," one of the girls said to the student on the bench, "may we ask you a question?"

These girls are part of the college ministry where my husband and I serve at our church. Every week, they and several others use their time between classes to walk around campus and share the gospel message with any student who will listen.

It's been such a blessing to see the boldness of these students and to hear their stories. But if you'd told me a year ago that this same group of students would be taking such risks, I probably would not have believed you.

There is wisdom in making plans. It's a good thing to think through all of your options and be prepared. But there's a limit. If we're honest, this idea of "don't make a move until you feel 100 percent safe, comfortable, and ready" can be paralyzing.

What does this obsession with safety and comfort sound like when there is an opportunity to witness?

"I *would* share the gospel, but first I need to grow more spiritually."

"I *would* share the gospel, but I don't know enough. What if I can't answer their questions?"

"I *would* share the gospel, but talking to people about religion is really outside of my comfort zone."

Fears, insecurities, and doubts keep us from taking the risk of obedience in our daily lives. But for the Christian, risk-taking is an essential part of gospel-living and disciple-making.

Think of Abraham, Moses, David, Samuel, Paul, Timothy, and countless others in the Bible who acted in obedience when, by the world's standards, the odds were most definitely against them. If they had not taken risks—if they had chosen to obey only after they felt ready or felt like it made sense—then the glory of God would not have been displayed in such prevalent, breathtaking ways.

First Corinthians 1:27-29 (ESV) tells us this in a beautiful way:

But God chose what is foolish in the world to shame the wise; God chose what is weak in the world to shame the strong; God chose what is low and despised in the world, even things that are not, to bring to nothing things that are, so that no human being might boast in the presence of God.

When God's people act in obedience in spite of feeling weak or unqualified, God's glory is magnified all the more.

The shift in our college ministry began when our pastor realized that our students were not sharing the gospel on a regular basis, and they used many of the above reasons to justify their inaction.

He began to hold weekly events on campus in which he would spend twenty to thirty minutes training students on a simple method of sharing the gospel. Then, they spent the next forty-five minutes to an hour going out on campus and *doing* it. First, the students would watch our pastor do it; then, one by one, the students tried it themselves.

In the beginning, our students were hesitant, uncomfortable, and terrified. Then one day, something amazing happened—a student came to know Christ.

And in that moment, a fire was ignited. More of our students began to show up at the weekly trainings. They started to gather in groups on other days of the week to share the gospel by themselves. More people became Christians, and our ministry's excitement was contagious.

Here is the incredible irony: the Christian who resists obedience and instead clings to comfort and security will usually find himself miserable and stagnant in his faith. But when we dare to obey and step out in faith, we experience intimacy with Christ and a trust in Him that deepens with every uncomfortable, cross-carrying risk.

The safest place for us is not within the confines of our comfort zone. Instead, we find true, eternal security within the shadow of our Father's wings (Psalm 63:7) and on the path of obedience lit by His perfect Word (Psalm 119:105).

When we take risks, do hard things, and step out in obedience, we will see our faith grow and His name glorified. And there is nothing more thrilling.

Prayer:

Father, Obedience can be so frightening. Please give me the strength to step out in boldness for You today. Help me remember that my safest place is not within my comfort zone, but in Your will. Please use me today so that others may see the greatness of

Your glory. Let my only boast be in Jesus Christ; make me more like You.

Questions:

1. Read Hebrews 11:8-10. In what ways did Abraham act in obedience? What motivated him to take such a risk?

2. Read 1 John 2:3-6. According to John, what is the proof that we truly know Christ and have a relationship with Him? What does this look like practically in everyday life?

3. Write down three ways you can step outside of your comfort zone and into obedience this week. Share your goals with a friend for accountability, and then write down what happens after each act of obedience.

The Power of Knowing
Introduction

What difference does it make to know that God is always with us and for us? That in the storms of life we can take refuge in Him? That He works in us, and that He has work for us? What is the power of knowing?

In this section of *The Power to Make a Difference*, the authors share stories and insights about the difference that knowing God and His Word has made in their lives, and the difference it can make in ours. They tell us how they relied on the truths and promises of God, and were helped, encouraged, or motivated to act in His name. They remind us of who God is, His deep love for us, and His great power that is exerted on our behalf. Some of them tell us ways that we can know God better, and what we will gain once we do.

> *We ... do not cease to pray for you ... that you may be filled with the knowledge of His will in all wisdom and spiritual understanding; that you may walk worthy of the Lord, fully pleasing Him, being fruitful in every good work and increasing in the knowledge of God.* (Colossians 1:9-10 NKJV)

Burlap Angel
by Dorcas Asercion Zuniga

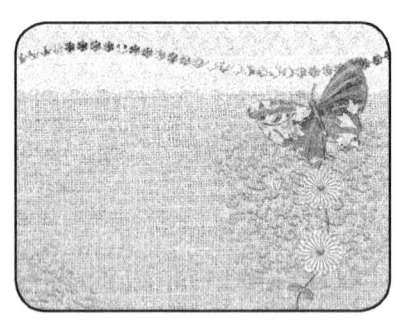

It started out as a fun craft for the school's holiday bazaar fundraiser. But for nine-year-old me, it quickly turned into a hopeless mess.

In our fourth-grade art class, my classmates and I learned how to stitch yarn onto a piece of burlap. Our simple designs were easy and fun to create. So when our teacher asked if any of us wanted to make a craft to be sold at the bazaar, I volunteered. I wanted to stitch an angel on a piece of burlap.

Mom and Dad were all for my project. Dad got the supplies I needed: white yarn, the right size needle, a wooden embroidery hoop, and a piece of burlap. After I drew an outline of an angel on the burlap, Mom helped me get started. Then she turned the needle over to me.

But things did not go as smoothly as I had imagined. I had to redo areas where there were gaps between the strands of yarn. Then the yarn became tangled and knotted. Time quickly slipped away from me. Suddenly the deadline to turn in all donations was the next day.

I held the piece of burlap in my hands. All I saw was matted yarn. I had no idea how to fix it. But because I had promised to turn in a craft, I had no choice but to submit my angel, knots and all. I put the burlap on my pillow and cried myself to sleep.

The next morning, I sat up in bed with puffy eyes and a heavy heart. Then I saw it, on my pillow where I had left it the night before. My angel—complete and beautiful. The gaps and knots were gone. New stitches blended with the ones I had made. And stitches of yarn outlined the pattern I had drawn to help the white angel stand out against the brown background of the burlap. My mother had come into my room after I had fallen asleep and worked through the night to fix my artwork. She completed the work that she had helped me begin. The lovely outcome became one of the star attractions at the school bazaar.

There would be many more "projects" that my mom would help me fix. But as I entered adulthood, I found that many of my feelings of inadequacy needed solutions beyond her loving touch. They needed the Hand of my Heavenly Father.

My struggles are not limited to my personal and professional life. There are too many times when I doubt my spiritual progress. Am I providing the nurturing and encouragement my son needs to grow in his spiritual walk? Am I giving the support my husband needs as he ministers to others? Am I living the life that is pleasing to Yahweh˚? Am I truly saved?

> *Being confident of this, that he who began a good work in you will carry it on to completion until the day of* [Messiah Yeshua˚]. (Philippians 1:6 NIV)

In his letter to the believers in Philippi, Paul assured them that Yahweh would continue the work of salvation in them that started when they received the Good News. The Philippians could rest in the knowledge that their salvation would reach completion when their Savior returned.

We have that same assurance. If we stumble during our faith walk, Yahweh will hold us up. When we have doubts, He will reassure us. Yahweh began His work in us when we received Yeshua Messiah as our Savior. And He always completes what He starts.

Part of our journey includes fulfilling the role for which Yahweh created us. In high school, Yahweh placed in my heart the desire to become a medical doctor. Although this was not my childhood dream, the calling grew stronger throughout college. But in medical school, I questioned if I had what it took to become a doctor. Then in residency, I struggled with doubts about my competency. During those moments of anxiety and fear, I would go to sleep not knowing what my future held. But Yahweh surrounded me with the love and support of family and friends and the ardent prayers of my mother and father. And through His grace, I completed my training.

> *For we are* [Yahweh's] *handiwork, created in* [Messiah Yeshua] *to do good works, which* [Yahweh] *prepared in advance for us to do.* (Ephesians 2:10 NIV)

Yahweh has a divine plan for each one of His children, and He puts in our hearts the desire to work toward His purpose. When we entrust ourselves to Him, we can be sure He will complete that work in our lives.

In my mother's hands, a piece of ordinary burlap became the background of a beautiful angel. The art was a work made with love. In the Hands of the One whose love is everlasting, our bodies made from dust are transformed into His masterpieces, destined to see the completion of His act of salvation when His Beloved Son returns to earth once more.

When we have the Son, we can be confident that Our Father will finish all the work He started within us.

Prayer:

Sovereign Yahweh, Take away the doubts that keep me from fully trusting that You will bring to completion Your purpose for my life. Thank You for the assurance of the blessed hope of salvation through Yeshua our Savior.

Questions:

1. Has there been a time when you questioned your salvation? What does 1 John 5:11-12 tell you about obtaining eternal life?

2. How does 2 Corinthians 4:7 encourage you when you feel inadequate in serving Yahweh?

3. In what situation will the promise in Philippians 1:6 help you continue onward in your faith walk?

---

*Author's Note: Yahweh is the Hebrew name of God the Father, as revealed to Moses in Exodus 3:15. Yeshua Messiah (HaMashiach) is the Hebrew name of Jesus Christ, our Risen Savior. Thank you for allowing me to share these special names with you.

Squashie Detour
by Dawn Linton

Filled with freedom and adventure, I began my first walk home from school alone. I detoured onto a narrow street lined with dull brick buildings and unwashed windows. The mysterious aroma of freshly baked cupcakes wafted through the air, flooding my senses, pulling me like a magnet until I stood in front of the Hostess Cupcake Factory and Delivery Center. How I longed for a taste! I wrapped my eight-year-old hand around the unpolished bronzed handle of the huge dull door. Using all of my small-sized strength, leaning back for leverage, grunting, and pulling, pulling, pulling … the door squeaked on its hinges and opened just enough for me to see inside.

"Come on in! Would you like a 'Squashie'?"

My eyes widened at the mountain of baked goods piled behind the friendly lady.

"What's a Squashie?" I asked timidly.

Squashies were double-packed baked goods, crushed at one end or right in the middle. She handed me a cellophane-wrapped duo of chocolate cupcakes with white cream filling in the middle, chocolate frosting, and a line of white cursive "e's" on top. From that moment on, I lived for the sound of the school bell, dismissing me to travel my secret detour. Every day I struggled to pull that big door open and yell, "Any Squashies today!!?"

To most, perhaps, "Squashie" was a name for things that were disqualified, of no value, damaged goods. But to me, Squashies were delightful gifts, better than anything imaginable. Squashies had flavor, they were fresh, and they were free!

Looking back now from an older and wiser perspective on my daily "Squashie Detour," I recognize that in my life, good things not yet imagined would be as surprising to me as the Hostess Cupcake Factory and Delivery Center was to a child with no money who loves cupcakes. Other certain happenings would threaten to make me damaged goods. But even as I meandered through twists and turns, God's profound and powerful hand was on me, and in His heart was a plan to fill my soul with more life than if I had never been crushed.

What does the Bible say about happenings that threaten to make you damaged goods? Ancient Hebrew writers tell of the Valley of the Balsam Trees, where gum-distilling "weepers" grow, releasing tears of gum. They called it the Valley of Baca, or weeping, symbolic for an experience of sorrow. There is *no shame* in being a "weeper." Crushing valleys are exhausting. They require caution to slow down and good counsel to make wise choices. In them, God calls you to take refuge.

Take Refuge

Running to God for refuge is not slipping and sliding on tears into the valley of despair, waiting for a miracle. Nor is it denial of pain or injustice. Taking refuge seldom provides escape on a bridge over troubled waters. To take refuge in God means trusting Him as a protected place until the disaster is over (Psalm 57:1-2). It is acknowledging that you cannot navigate this on your own. You may run to Him in fear, but you settle with Him in *rest*. Refuge is a place of confiding in God and waiting until He gives you guidance and courage for the next step.

Why Take Refuge?

Take refuge because God is strong and He is good (Nahum 1:7). He will never leave you (Hebrews 13:5). Take refuge in Him because your trust will activate a cosmic plan of redemption that brings value from pain (Romans 8:28). Take refuge so that what happens to you does not become your identity, blinding you to treasure that does not exist apart from trouble (Isaiah 45:3). Take refuge until you are infused with courage to move forward with God. Eventually, you will stand together with the valley in rear view, equipped with greater insight, integrity, and influence (Jeremiah 29:11).

Treasure from trouble may include a new life path, increased empathy, unexpected opportunity, emotional freedom, greater faith, or humility. When you develop a history of valley walks with God, you will experience the power of redemption.

How do you recalibrate your heart when a "Squashie Detour" leads to a daunting valley? How do you move from paralysis to *hope*? How do you reposition yourself for redemption?

How to Take Refuge

1. MOURN: Resist the pressure to make others feel better by moving forward too quickly. Don't dry your tears too soon (Matthew 5:4). The valley is a journey, and "the best way out is always through."[1]

2. PRAY: Be honest with God. Wrestle with Him (Psalm 13:2). Pour out your heart to Him (Psalm 62:7-8).

3. TRUST: Put your hand into the hand of God and walk with Him. Learn what He will teach you about Himself (Matthew 11:28-30) and about yourself (Psalm 139:23). Choose to trust Him (Proverbs 3:5-6).

4. HAVE HOPE: Look for evidence that God is with you (John 14:21). Then thank Him, and call no good thing a coincidence (2 Chronicles 16:9).

You may not know how you landed in a valley, how long you'll be there, or how to get out. But know this: you have the option to trust God, to set your heart on movement, and to take safe refuge while you do.

Blessed are those whose strength is in you, whose hearts are set on pilgrimage. As they pass through the Valley of Baka, they make it a place of springs. (Psalm 84:5-6 NIV)

Prayer:

Lord, I'm afraid. I've heard You can be trusted, I've learned stories of Your faithfulness, and I've memorized Scripture. Yet, I am full of doubt as I face this valley. Please help my unbelief, and grant me the grace to walk with You and to trust Your promises. Thank You for providing safe refuge. Amen.

Questions:

1. Can you think of an example of a "Squashie" experience that threatened to damage you, but instead resulted in something you delight in?

2. Which guideline on how to take refuge is most difficult for you? Memorize one of the Scripture verses listed that encourages you.

3. How could taking refuge in God transform unwanted detours from wasted paths into intentional journeys of new vistas? Can you think of any examples in the Bible? In your own experiences?

---

1. Robert Frost, "A Servant to Servants," line 56, from *North of Boston* (1915), https://www.bartleby.com/118/9.html.

Because I'm Convinced
by Mary Albers Felkins

*For I am convinced that neither death nor life,
neither angels nor demons,
neither the present nor the future,
nor any powers, neither height nor depth,
nor anything else in all creation,
will be able to separate us from the love of God
that is in Christ Jesus our Lord.*
(Romans 8:38-39 NIV®)

An unexpected announcement had me reeling. The classic blindside. For about twenty-four hours afterward, I indulged in a good ole' pity party. Then I rose above it, refreshed and strengthened, and far more equipped.

Easy? Not at all.

Then how?

I've become convinced of God's inseparable love.

Knowing—and being convinced—that nothing within or without, above or below, past or present can separate me from the love of God, is powerful. It does me no good if I know the truth of God's word but refuse to apply it to my circumstances. To doubt God's love hinders my ability to impact the world for Jesus.

When faced with hardship, we can either allow it to unravel us or embrace the good in it, fully armed with truth …

For I am convinced that [nothing] will be able to separate us from the love of God that is in Christ Jesus our Lord.

This blessed assurance in Romans leaves no wiggle room for exceptions.

The world hates. The world rejects. The world is unwelcoming. The world zips from one newsworthy item to the next and, just as quickly, forgets. Like Paul, we must become convinced that, dead in sin or alive in Christ, we are wanted and loved by God (even when we don't love Him back).

To be convinced of God's love requires us to pursue intimate knowledge of Jesus who said, *I am the way and the truth and the life. No one comes to the Father except through me* (John 14:6).

But at some point in our life, we may have allowed ourselves to become wrongly convinced that our mistakes—past, present, future—have made us unlovable. Unredeemable. Not good enough. Meant for rejection.

Knowing and embracing the truth—that nothing can separate us from the love of God—is essential fuel for the journey. Otherwise, we'll crumble when the added weight of hardship rests on our shoulders and life won't let up.

Though He slay me, yet will I hope in Him … this will turn out for my deliverance. (Job 13:15-16)

- When rejection hits, there's power in knowing we can't be separated from God's love.

- When tragedy strikes, there's power in knowing God is wholly good and *all the ways of the LORD are loving and faithful toward those who keep … his covenant* (Psalm 25:10).

- When fear of uncertainty niggles into our mind, there's power in knowing God's love will drive it out and break the stronghold. *And so we know and rely on the love God has for us. God is love ... There is no fear in love. But perfect love drives out fear* (I John 4:16, 18).

- When blindsided by loss, there's power in knowing **God has said, "Never will I leave you; never will I forsake you"** (Hebrews 13:5).

Points to Ponder:

Take time to know the Truth. *You will know the truth, and the truth will set you free* (John 8:32). There's no convincing us of something we don't know in the first place. God has blessed us with His Spirit-breathed revelation of truth in Scripture. We should prioritize time with God, ask Him to illuminate His word, and let it become etched in our hearts. All things can then be measured against it, tested for accuracy.

Let hardship teach. Being a convinced Christian typically comes through difficulties, the wise engineering of circumstances by our sovereign God whereby Scripture becomes more precious to us. How else will we know the power of healing if we're not injured? Or that we are loved by God if not rejected at times? Or that we are fully known by God unless we've felt invisible?

Allow ourselves to be convinced. Sometimes we remain unconvinced of His love because we've kept a tight fist about a matter, unwilling to accept the truth in His word. Ask God for deliverance from having been convinced of a lie over the truth about ourselves and our circumstances.

For I am convinced that [nothing] will be able to separate us from the love of God that is in Christ Jesus our Lord.

The more convinced we become of His inseparable love, the stronger our faith and the greater difference we can make in the world.

Of what are you fully convinced? Will it sustain you through the hardships of life?

Prayer:

Lord, You give us the gift of Your perfect Word. You lavish us with unmerited grace, knowledge of Your inseparable love, and the ability to become convinced of it. May this strengthen and sustain us through and beyond hardship so that the world may know Your love.

Questions:

1. Are you ever tempted to believe the lie that God doesn't love you?

2. If so, what helps to convince you of the truth again? If not, what keeps you steadfast?

3. Of the four bullet points in the study, which "power of knowing" statement is the most meaningful to you?

4. Which of the three "Points to Ponder" might be the most effective in your life right now?

---

*All Scripture verses are taken from the NIV.

Delectable
by Barb Fox

Southern hospitality revolves around delicious food presented in a delectable manner.

When I graduated from college, I moved to Georgia and soon faced a crisis. I thought knowing how to cook meant simply being able to read recipes and measure ingredients. I soon discovered it also required interpreting ambiguous terms like "until firm," "a pinch," and "al dente." In addition, apparently a young woman is supposed to own things that I'd never heard of like ramekins and trifle bowls. Fortunately, I had a mother and some church friends who shared their knowledge, and my kitchen disasters began waning in frequency.

Growing in knowledge is helpful in cooking, but also in our Christian walk.

Epaphras told Paul about new converts in the city of Colosse who loved God and their fellow saints. Paul recognized that these young believers needed to grow in their knowledge of God. They understood the basics, much as I knew the basics of cooking, but partial knowledge can sometimes lead to misinterpretations and mistakes.

As a spiritual mentor, Paul immediately set the example for them. First and foremost, he brought their need to God through prayer. Beginning on the day he learned about these Corinthian Christians, he interceded for them. Not once, not twice, but unceasingly. His primary prayer was that they *be filled with the knowledge of His will in all wisdom and spiritual understanding* (Colossians 1:9 NKJV*).

The new believers obviously knew the basics. Paul's letter affirmed that they understood terms like the Father, the Lord Jesus Christ, and the Spirit, and that they had faith in the truth of the gospel. They already knew everything they needed for salvation, but Paul prayed for something more—that their knowledge of God's will be full in the two practical aspects of wisdom and spiritual understanding.

Wisdom is knowing what to do with existing knowledge, in other words, how to take the next step. To be filled with head knowledge is not the same as acting in faith. Paul prayed for these people to have all wisdom, so they would know what to do in all circumstances.

Spiritual understanding involves being able to put knowledge in context and apply meaning to it. Jesus often illuminated Old Testament passages by putting them in the context of daily living. He helped His listeners understand how to love their neighbor through the parable of the good Samaritan (Luke 10:25-37) and to understand the concept of generous giving through the example of a widow who dropped two tiny coins into the temple treasury (Luke 21:1-4). Paul prayed that the Colossians would have a complete and full understanding of spiritual matters as they relate to God's will.

The power of this type of knowledge and the associated understanding and wisdom are outlined in Colossians 1:10-11, which enumerates at least four incredible blessings.

> *[We ask] that you may walk worthy of the Lord, fully pleasing Him, being fruitful in every good work and increasing in the knowledge of God; strengthened with all might, according to His glorious power, for all patience and longsuffering with joy.*

First, this knowledge would enable them to *walk worthy of the Lord, fully pleasing Him* (v.10). Young children will do almost anything to please their parents. What an encouragement to these young children of God, for Paul to assure them that growing in knowledge would help them to please God and walk in a way that would bring honor to His name.

Secondly, this knowledge would help them to be *fruitful in every good work* (v.10). When my cooking skills improved, I began to share God's love by serving meals to shut-ins, new mothers, and grieving friends. Knowing God's will for us allows us even greater servant opportunities like sharing the gospel or helping a person in need. Titus 3:14 (NASB) states, *Our people must also learn to engage in good deeds to meet pressing needs, so that they will not be unfruitful.*

Third, knowing God's will compels us to lead a changed life, which leads to the person *increasing in the knowledge of God* (v.10). Knowing a little is the first step to learning a lot. Knowing the difference between a teaspoon and a tablespoon is a good start for cooking, but chefs who create masterpieces have attended formal training, spent years learning under others as a sous-chef, and continue growing in their skills every year. Like these chefs, the fruit we bear as Christians grows as each new piece of knowledge builds on what we have learned before.

Knowing God's will, understanding it, and walking in it, is immeasurably more interesting than cooking. It is an ever-rewarding and never-ending delight. Everything learned about His will leads to a deeper knowledge of Him. For example, knowing that He desires to forgive sinners, helps His people know and understand even more about His perfect love.

Fourth, the knowers will be *strengthened with all might, according to His glorious power, for all patience and longsuffering with joy* (v.11). Knowing God better paves the way for God's blessings to flow more freely. These Colossians, like us, would face challenges that would require patience and forbearance. Through Paul's inspired words, God communicated that they would receive strength from His infinite power source not only to endure the trials, but to celebrate them with joy.

As I think back to those days when I knew little about cooking, I recall many failures in the kitchen. Smoke alarms. Using Jif® the peanut butter, in place of Jiffy® the all-purpose baking mix. Cooking a frozen pizza with the cardboard circle underneath it. But as my knowledge increased, so did my understanding. Eventually I understood that "until browned" meant something different depending on whether I was cooking a cut of beef or a batch of cookies. And my wisdom also increased. For example, I started using a timer to remind me to remove items from the oven. I relied on friends to educate me and steer me in the right direction. Soon I was serving fragrant homemade bread from scratch.

These verses to the Corinthians of the first century offer so much more than an impressive dinner or fancy dessert. Paul asked that Christ-followers be filled with a knowledge of God's will that was practical and useful—knowledge that would enable them to live a life that glorified God and produced a bountiful harvest. What a glorious motivator it is to know that God Himself will supply all that is needed to produce a delectable life.

Prayer:

Dear God, You are the source of all good things. Help me to know You and Your will. I trust You to fulfill Your promises of giving me wisdom and strength to act in ways that please You. I look forward to a rich life that honors You and blesses others, one full of the good works You planned for me before I was even born. Amen.

Questions:

1. What is one thing you "know" about God's will in your life today?

2. What is one way that knowledge has increased your understanding of God's character?

3. How has this knowledge changed your actions or attitudes?

*All Scripture verses are taken from the NKJV unless otherwise indicated.

Knowing God Is with Me
by Jenifer Kitchens

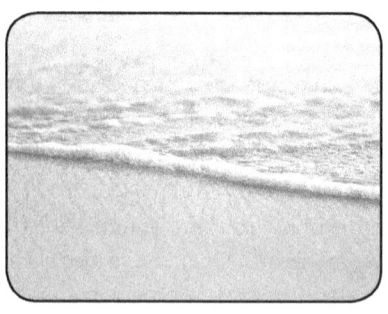

My family went to the beach this past summer. We have three kids, and each had a different response to the ocean.

Our ten-year-old daughter is a confident swimmer and remembered playing in the ocean a few years ago. She was eager to run to the waves and submerge herself, playing with the pull of the tide.

Our not quite one-year-old was experiencing the surf and sand for the first time, and when holding our hands, he wanted to explore these new sensations as much as possible. He would lean towards the water, not realizing its power or potential danger.

Our six-year-old remembered the waves from before. Not being a confident swimmer, her memory was one of being blindsided by a huge wave that knocked her out of the grasp of her grandmother, overwhelmed her, and scared her. Her fear caused her to be quite content staying on the sand digging holes. A time or two, I put her on my hip and waded out into waist-high water, asking her to trust me as we jumped waves together. I absolutely had her. The waves weren't high that day and I easily kept her head above water. She knew what could happen, though, and she never relaxed or truly enjoyed the time we were spending together.

Isaiah 41 prophesies the return of the Hebrew people to Jerusalem under King Cyrus. God knew that the Jews would be fearful at the prospect of this. They were God's people but they had not grown up in the land promised to them. They would be going somewhere they had never been. They would be experiencing resistance from people around them. They didn't know what they would find. Creating a new life for themselves and their children was daunting. God knew the hearts of His people and before they even set out for this place, He gave words to encourage them. In Isaiah 41:10 (NASB), God gives this truth—for us, too—to know and embrace:

Do not fear, for I am with you;
Do not anxiously look about you, for I am your God.
I will strengthen you, surely I will help you,
Surely I will uphold you with My righteous right hand.

It is so reassuring to know that God is with me. Too often, I find myself like my middle child in my relationship with my Heavenly Father—so very afraid of what could happen and not trusting His absolute authority and power in every situation. I find myself, a wife of fifteen years and parent of three kids, looking around for the adult to step up and handle the situation instead of walking confidently through situations because I know God is with me. And when God says, *I am with you*, He used the same name He gave to Moses at the burning bush. God who revealed His power through the plagues, who protected His people by parting the Red Sea, and who provided by sending manna and quail, is with you.

God shows us that He knows us well when He reminds us not to look around. He knows we get distracted, we try to compare ourselves with others, we look for where the next attack will come from. We really need to just focus on Him, remind ourselves that no person and no situation compares to Him, and rest in Him.

God promises to strengthen us. How much stronger than us is He? His promise to help us is a game changer ... if we will trust His ways. I tend to try to handle things my way, with what I am capable of. I'm really not capable of much. Actually, I'm not capable of anything but messing things up. I need His strength. I need His help because I need to know what to do and where to go.

Surely I will uphold you with my righteous right hand. I'm so glad that God has a hold on me and it's not up to me to hold on to Him. I'm weak. He reminds us, though, that His hand is righteous. He will come to our rescue and even pull us out of our sin, but He won't help us to continue in that sin. We must be willing to let go of what separates us from God, those things which, if we're honest with ourselves, may have contributed to our needing His deliverance.

We don't have to rely on ourselves. We can rest in Him, knowing that He is with us. What a delight it is to know we are in the omnipotent arms of our Heavenly Father when the waves of life surround us.

Prayer:

You, God, are always with me. Please forgive me when I get distracted and look other places than You for help. I declare my dependence on You. Help me to live resting in the assurance of Your presence no matter what my circumstances are.

Questions:

1. My kids can't believe there are things that grownups are scared of. I told them there were, but I had a hard time putting those ideas into terms they could understand. Can you put your fears into words?

2. God has revealed Himself through His Word. What events in the Bible communicate character traits of God that you are so thankful for?

3. God says not to *anxiously look about you*. What distracts you from focusing on God?

4. God will uphold us with His *righteous right hand*. His righteousness draws a stark comparison to our unrighteousness. Is there any sin separating you from God? If so, are you willing to let go of it? Do it not so He will save you, but because you realize you need to let go of it and cling to God.

Getting to Know You
by Brad Simon

This is eternal life: that they may know you,
the only true God.
(John 17:3 CSB)

As I read those familiar words from the prayer of Jesus, there was something different. As I sat that morning in my recliner, my gaze lifted from the page of my Bible to the picture of Abraham Lincoln hanging on my office wall. Growing up in Illinois, Abe Lincoln was my favorite person of history. I have read and studied many books about Lincoln. Several times I toured the reconstructed town of New Salem where he lived as a young man, and I have visited his home and law office in Springfield. As a Boy Scout, I hiked the 21-mile Lincoln Trail, the route he traveled as a young statesman from New Salem to Springfield. While I know a lot about Abraham Lincoln, I cannot say that I know him.

As Christians we listen to sermons and attend Bible studies. We learn all about the attributes of God and all the things that God has done. We may know a lot about God, but do we truly know Him? Jesus said we are to know God, not just know about Him. The omnipotent, omniscient, omnipresent God, the creator of the universe, desires for us to know Him!

When I was first dating my wife Debbie, we lived in different cities. Every night I would wait until 11 pm when the long distant rates went down to call her at her home. I could have spoken to her sister or brother and learned a lot about Debbie. I could have talked to her parents and heard many stories about her. But I didn't want to talk to any of them; I wanted to speak with her. I did not just want to know about her; I wanted to know her.

Studying the attributes of God is beneficial. Listening to others tell us about God is valuable. Reading stories about what God has done is worthwhile. But none of them compare to getting to know Him personally. And how can you get to know Him? The same way I got to know my wife—you talk to Him.

The Apostle Paul said, *"Rejoice always, pray constantly, give thanks in everything; for this is God's will for you in Christ Jesus"* (1 Thessalonians 5:16-18 CSB). There is no asterisk after that verse that says, "unless you are really busy." (I know because I've looked!) We are to *pray constantly* (CSB), *pray without ceasing* (ESV), *pray continually* (NIV), *never stop praying* (NLT), *always keep on praying* (TLB).

All of us spend time every day talking to ourselves; some of us even argue with ourselves. How much more profitable that time would be if we spent it talking with God.

When you are driving down the street you can spend time talking with God. (You don't have to always bow your head and close your eyes when you pray). While you are getting dressed, when you are waiting for an appointment, when you are lying in bed trying to fall asleep. Well, you get the idea, anytime you are alone with your thoughts is the perfect time to talk with your Father in Heaven.

Then when you have talked with God, really listen to Him as you read His word. The apostle Paul said, *"Let the word of Christ dwell in you richly"* (Colossians 3:16 ESV). We should not read our Bible just to check off a list that we read our chapter for the day; we are to let the words we read "dwell" in us.

When Joshua took over the leadership of Israel after the death of Moses, God told him:

> *"This book of instruction must not depart from your mouth; you are to meditate on it day and night so that you may carefully observe everything written in it. For then you will prosper and succeed in whatever you do."* (Joshua 1:8 CSB)

Did you catch that? We are to *carefully observe everything written* in our Bible and we do that when we *meditate on it day and night*. As we listen to what God has to say and continually think about those words throughout our day, we get to know Him—not just know about Him.

The apostle John provides one final step in getting to know God—that of obedience to Him. In his first letter, John writes, *This is how we know that we know him: if we keep his commands. The one who says, "I have come to know him," and yet doesn't keep his commands, is a liar, and the truth is not in him* (1 John 2:3-4 CSB).

James, the half-brother of Jesus and leader in the church at Jerusalem, provides the following insight.

> *Be doers of the word and not hearers only, deceiving yourselves. Because if anyone is a hearer of the word and not a doer, he is like someone looking at his own face in a mirror. For he looks at himself, goes away, and immediately forgets what kind of person he was. But the one who looks intently into the perfect law of freedom and perseveres in it, and is not a forgetful hearer but a doer who works—this person will be blessed in what he does.* (James 1:22-25 CSB)

Anyone who wants to know God, to walk closely with Him, must obey Him. As we listen to God speak to us through the Scriptures we read, we need to conform our lives to what He says. It is not possible to develop a close relationship with God without our obedience.

Late in his life the apostle Paul wrote, *I also consider everything to be a loss in view of the surpassing value of knowing Christ Jesus my Lord. … My goal is to know him and the power of his resurrection* (Philippians 3:8, 10 CSB). Just think of all the missionary journeys Paul went on, all the churches he started, all the individuals he led to salvation, all the leaders he discipled, all the people he ministered to, and he considered all that to be a loss compared to the surpassing value of knowing Christ Jesus!

Paul is not saying that his ministry was unimportant, but that in comparison, having a personal intimate relationship with God was far more imperative. Knowing God, not just knowing about Him, provides the Christian the power needed to do ministry. May we, like the apostle Paul, make it our goal in life to get to know God.

Prayer:

Dear Heavenly Father, Forgive us for our apathy toward You. Let us not be content with just a saving knowledge of You. May we not become complacent in our lives, but may we take the time to talk with You and listen to You as we read from Your word. May we ever strive to get to know You better and grow closer to You as we walk with You throughout our daily lives. In the powerful name of Jesus, we pray these things. Amen.

Questions:

1. Is your current relationship with God best described as with someone you know or with a person you know about?

2. What time of day is best for you to spend time alone with God? Are you committed to meet at that time with Him daily?

3. Which of the three steps above—talking with God, listening to Him as you read His word, or obeying Him—do you need to work on the most?

4. What specific things will you commit to do to improve in this area?

5. Read John 14:21. What can we do to show God that we love Him, and what is His response to that?

Knowing That God Is Trustworthy
by Connie Wohlford

It was dusk when I walked into our house and a strange, almost eerie atmosphere thickened as I entered the family room. No one was there. I had been away for two days and expected to come home and hear TV noise, talking, and maybe even our two young sons arguing over some trivial matter.

But no—nothing. I walked to the far end of the room and lowered myself into a chair I loved but rarely took time to occupy. I sat, peering into the quiet space that was usually alive with activity on a Sunday evening. As I sat, I wondered, and an uneasy sense of foreboding came over me.

Where were my husband and sons? Why was there no note left for me, explaining their absence? (Cell phones were not yet a part of our lives.)

Suddenly, the ringing of our telephone broke through the haunting silence.

"Hello."

Relieved to hear my husband's voice, I listened.

"Hey, Honey, we're at Sonny's house and will be home in a few minutes."

His voice didn't seem quite normal so I pressed him.

"What's going on?"

"We had a car wreck, but we're all fine. Sonny's bringing us home. I'll tell you about it when I get there."

"When did it happen?" I inquired.

"A couple hours ago. We'll see you in a few minutes."

We said goodbyes, and I went back to the chair and sat down. My mind was racing and flashed back to my prayer encounter a couple of hours earlier.

With vivid recall, I reflected on the prompting to pray for my family at just the time the wreck had occurred.

While traveling home with friends from a church gathering, we stopped to eat at a restaurant in Mount Airy, North Carolina. Just as I sat down with my food, I heard the Holy Spirit speak to my own spirit. It was clear and undeniable.

"Pray for your family."

That's it—just four words. But I knew I was hearing from God.

A wave of urgency came over me. I felt my heart pounding in my chest and sat there, silently praying fervently for my family. I had no idea why, but I knew that God knew. After a brief time, I felt God's peace and ate dinner with my companions. I told no one of the conundrum stirring in my gut. For the rest of the trip questions raced through my mind, yet I was confident that God had the answers and had things under control.

So, I sat in the chair, immobilized by the words of my husband.

My pondering and prayers of gratitude were interrupted by the opening of the door and our boys rushing in to tell me all about their wild experience, with my husband, Guy, not far behind. As I listened, I realized that their ordeal was more harrowing than I had even imagined.

A friend had taken them to a nearby town where Guy purchased an older model Volkswagen Bug. He and the boys were traveling home in it when one of the tires blew out, sending the vehicle hurling over an embankment on the opposite side of the road, missing oncoming traffic.

Down the one hundred plus foot drop they went, overturning at least three times and coming to rest on the car's roof. Unharmed, the three climbed out of the gnarled VW through a broken window. Immediately, our older son, who was nine years old, ran back up the steep hill and across to the other side of the road, paying no attention to oncoming traffic in either direction. Matter of fact, a few days later, someone told me they were driving along that road and had seen a child dart across, not realizing who or why.

The excited youngster told us he was running because he feared the car was about to blow up. After all, that's what always happens in movies and TV shows.

I drew my little boys tight against my chest and tearfully thanked God for protecting these precious ones. I stood and gave Guy a lingering hug. He commented that he didn't understand my tears since they were all okay. Well, that's my Guy.

Needless to say, we were all beyond grateful. The thought of the tragedy that came so near to our family was too overwhelming to dwell on.

What if they had hit another vehicle head-on?

What if our car had exploded with them inside?

What if I had not stopped and prayed the moment God told me to do so?

What if God did not communicate with His people?

What if God was not trustworthy?

The what-ifs can be unnerving. But the knowing brings peace that passes understanding.

God knows me and my family, and He loves each of us with unfailing love. On the flip side, I know my God. I know He is trustworthy. The more I learn about Him the better I get to know Him personally. The better I get to know Him, the more I trust Him.

Many years have gone by since the wreck in the VW, and I'm still in awe of God and how He rescued my family from possible death or serious injury. I'm also in awe of how He spoke to me and told me to pray for them at that very moment. Knowing God and the assurance that He knows all things are some of the most comforting realities of walking with the Lord. Knowing His voice when He speaks is not only thrilling, but can even be a matter of life and death.

When distress comes along, I often reassure myself and others with these words, "God knows, God loves, and God cares." Knowing this to be true, in the depths of our being, prepares us to face whatever difficulties life hurls at us.

I'm grateful to serve a God who knows me—a God who, through His Word, I can know. We are well acquainted with each other. He may not always find me trustworthy but I can certainly always trust Him. I rejoice with King David for God's intimate knowledge and understanding of me and everything about me, as he portrayed in Psalm 139.

> *O LORD, You have searched me and known me.*
> *You know my sitting down and my rising up;*
> *You understand my thought afar off.*
> *You comprehend my path and my lying down,*
> *and are acquainted with all my ways.*
> (Psalm 139:1-3 NKJV)

Prayer:

Oh God, Life is full of uncertainties, and one never knows what awaits around the next corner—good or bad. But thank You, Father, that You know. And thank You that You care and You love me with unconditional and unfailing love. Your arms are not so short that You're unable to reach down and do mighty things on my behalf. Help me, O Lord, to confidently know this and trust You in all that pertains to my life. With a grateful heart, I praise You and thank You. In Jesus' name, Amen.

Questions:

1. Have you ever been told by the Holy Spirit or felt a strong urge, to pray for someone or a situation? Explain the situation and how you responded.

2. What are some attributes of God that you are confident of and grateful to know?

3. Read Psalm 139, and write notes or highlights that are the most meaningful to you.

4. Write out these passages:
    Exodus 3:7
    John 8:31-32

The Architect Knows
by Ron Gallagher

During a trip to Nashville, Tennessee last year, someone reflected on the building boom going on at the time. He said there were more building cranes erected and working there than any city in the country. I didn't Google it to fact-check his story, but it was interesting to see all those huge booms that seemed to be rising up everywhere we looked.

Huge construction cranes are fascinating. One was working on a large project adjacent to my wife's office a couple of years ago, and I came close enough every day to watch the giant machine work. It was hypnotic, and I couldn't help pondering the importance of the crane's role in building that structure. The architect was using a modular design. Pre-formed sections of concrete and masonry were trucked in to the site one piece at a time. Huge sections of walls and concrete floors were lifted off the trucks by that crane and carefully lowered into place where they almost instantly became a finished part of the building.

An Incredible Show ~

I was freshly astonished every time I stopped to watch. The weight that crane could lift was incredible. Not just tons, but hundreds of tons were picked up as easily as I might pick up a piece of balsa wood. Lifting those pieces and carrying them to the place they needed to go by human strength alone would be beyond impossible. Even if the "Incredible Hulk" was real, he couldn't get mad enough or turn green enough to accomplish a feat like that. When I considered the contrast between the tonnage being lifted and the personal effort exerted by the operator, it was like beholding something miraculous.

I had no idea what kind of crane I was watching, but that didn't matter. Regardless of the manufacturer, it was obviously a marvel of precision engineering, a carefully designed set of mechanical and hydraulic systems and subsystems. It included all kinds of parts made from a variety of materials and assembled by a host of different people with different skills and abilities. This conglomeration of diverse elements and materials was ultimately connected in an interdependent relationship. Properly activated and directed, they represented a potential for power that is genuinely awesome.

Working with Limited Knowledge ~

I could see the operator at work, and while his firsthand knowledge of crane design would certainly have exceeded mine, it's doubtful he could have designed and built one. Even if he had the basic shell to begin with, multitudes of complex mathematical, mechanical, and geometric formulas would be required to compute and construct the necessary boom length, optimum lift angles, number of cables, pulleys, and effective counter weights. He'd have to determine the number and size of hydraulic cylinders and accompanying diesel power. Yet in spite of not knowing all that stuff, there he sat, manipulating with ease a huge machine he did not and could not personally create, lifting things he would be powerless to move on his own.

Sometimes simple and obvious things can have profound implications, like the awareness that the operator I was watching didn't have to know everything about how the crane's power worked in order to know how to work with its power. He was building something massive, but he didn't have to memorize the blueprints of the structure to do his job. He may have been totally inept at doing the interior finish work and clueless about plumbing, and it wouldn't have mattered. All that mattered to him was properly handling the controls of that crane.

A Different Kind of Artistry ~

What made him valuable was knowing how cranes work, not how to build one. He needed to know which lever moves what, and which pedal controls which motion. He had to learn where to put his hands and feet and how much pressure to exert where, and when—simple movements, but vital when in contact with those controls. The end result was mesmerizing. He moved that huge apparatus with the grace and dexterity of an artist, slipping those tons of concrete and steel into place with a simple touch of his fingers. I had no idea what his name was, or how he learned to do what he did so well—and the anonymity of it all made me kind of sad.

The building's all done now—crane's gone, street's quiet. No sign remains to show that a crane was ever there, except all that concrete and steel rising up from the earth. There's no plaque with the operator's name, and nothing to tell what his role was in its construction. The occupants are all concerned with other things and neither know nor care. I'll bet the architect would care, though, and he would be proud. If he could have sat there with me in the car that day and watched his operator fit those huge pieces into place, he wouldn't have cared whether or not the guy could design and build a crane by himself.

A Lesson in Profound Simplicity ~

Some lessons seem to rise up from nowhere and grip my heart, like the one the crane operator taught me. I don't have to know everything in order to do what I'm sent to do. Just like the crane operator, in my own strength alone, the tasks I'm sent to do are impossible—but the power source I'm offered is mind-boggling. It isn't my creation, and I don't fully understand all of the intricacies, and that's OK, because I don't have to. For God to do *exceedingly abundantly above all that [I] ask or think* (Ephesians 3:20 NKJV), does not require superhuman effort on my part. It's accomplished *according to the power that works in [me]* (Eph 3:20 NKJV). My part in God's plan is not all that complicated.

Like my teacher, the crane operator, demonstrated, sometimes doing things that are overwhelming is as simple as putting our hands and feet in the right places, and keeping our eyes focused on the task at hand. We don't need to know all the formulas. If we just put our hands and feet where God directs us, and move them the way He said we should, we might see loads being lifted and things being built that astound those who are watching. And if they never know our name or what we did, that's OK, too. It won't diminish in the least the importance of our contribution—and besides, the Architect knows ... and He won't forget.

Prayer:

Father, Thank You for designing the blueprints of a blessed life with You and for You. Direct our efforts as we work in Your power and strength. Help us to make a difference in the world according to Your design. In Jesus' name, Amen.

Questions:

1. What power does the gospel of Jesus Christ have, according to Romans 1:16?

2. What did Jesus instruct us to do with it, in Matthew 28:19-20?

3. In Matthew 14:28-31, why did Peter begin to sink?

4. According to Hebrews 13:20-21, who works in us, how did He demonstrate His great power, and what does He enable us to do?

5. What encouragement does 1 Corinthians 15:58 give us?

Knowing Our Identity
by Jennifer DeFrates

A small flickering bulb lit everything but the corners of the nursery with a warm glow. In the mahogany glider, I rocked slowly. My once empty arms, which had ached more than a decade for a child, were finally full. Her soft baby scent etched itself into my memory.

I could not imagine loving her any more if I had given birth to her myself. I still can't.

But would she feel that loved? Would she see in herself the immeasurable worth and potential that I do?

Would she find her identity in the broken part of her story or the redeemed part?

Our identity is the root of what value we believe we have. While we know that her birthmother carefully crafted an adoption plan out of love, I worried that she would feel rejected, which could create an identity based on trauma and abandonment, leading her to grow up in shame and despair.

So many nights, I have rocked and prayed for her heart as an adopted child.

We had created a small photo storybook for her even though she was far too young to understand its pages. Each page reminded her that we would love her, encourage her, and support her. Photographs of my husband or me holding her, rocking her, or tickling her accompanied each paragraph.

The last page promised that we would always be family with a picture of the three of us standing with the judge, finalizing her adoption. As I read that page to her, I wondered if she would ever feel less than because she was *only* adopted.

While the social worker had assured us that telling her from the beginning, from before she could even understand, was the right decision, I worried that knowing would always be the tiniest of walls between us, a sliver of distance because she was not biologically ours.

Would she feel different from other children? Would she know what an incredible answer to prayer she is to us, how special she is?

Many nights as she grew, our bedtime stories told tales of kangaroos who adopted wee lambs, or foxes who waited for just the right fox child to complete their family.

Later, we told our sweet girl the story of the many ways God orchestrated her adoption. Before we even knew she existed, God had been working out the details of bringing her into our family.

The very week I sobbed on my bed praying to God for a child, wondering if we would ever find a way to adopt, she was conceived. As I lay there surrendering my desires, asking God to take them away or refocus my heart if parenting wasn't in His plans, He was knitting her together.

Months later, we were finally on the waiting list hoping a birthmother would choose us. Yet, the waiting was hard. One morning, I prayed surrendering the wait to God, asking Him to bless the waiting and give me a heart to enjoy it.

My phone rang an hour and a half later. "Mrs. DeFrates, we have a match! A baby girl due in June."

Once when she was around five, she asked where did she come from if she didn't grow in my tummy. I answered, "You grew in my heart, but your birthmother's tummy. God knew that I couldn't carry you in my body, but He always had a plan to bring you into our family from long before you were born."

And through stories of God's sweet faithfulness to her and to us, being adopted has become symbolic of God's incredible love for her.

Instead of abandoned, given up, or different, her identity became the child whose future God intricately planned. He reached out of heaven to bless her, and our family through her, in a unique way.

Her identity never was solely as my daughter, but always rested in Him first because of her adoption, just as my identity rests in Him as His daughter because of my adoption in Christ Jesus.

And God thought the lesson of adoption was so important, He wrote it in His word for us all.

> *Blessed be the God and Father of our Lord Jesus Christ, who has blessed us in Christ with every spiritual blessing in the heavenly places, even as he chose us in him before the foundation of the world, that we should be holy and blameless before him. In love he predestined us for adoption to himself as sons through Jesus Christ … In him we have redemption through his blood, the forgiveness of our trespasses, according to the riches of his grace, which he lavished upon us, in all wisdom and insight.* (Ephesians 1:3-5, 7-8 ESV)

Before the foundation of the world, God chose me, and everyone who believes in Jesus, for adoption into His family. He chose us for redemption and holiness.

I don't have to feel less than or left out when the world says, "You're different." I don't have to operate in the world without a true sense of my worth.

We are redeemed through Christ and forgiven as *sons*. We share with Christ in God's kingdom as children, not as slaves or servants.

My daughter needed an identity. Before she was even born, she had experienced loss and trauma and rejection, as we do everyday in this world.

Sometimes, she gets sad about the biological family she will never know, but she takes comfort in her adoptive families, both ours and God's.

Adoption is such a powerful message for me too. When I'm rejected, I have power in knowing my identity as a child of God. When I face persecution or trials, I have freedom in my identity as blameless, holy, and forgiven.

When I worry about what tomorrow will bring, I know God lavishes the riches of His grace upon me. I don't need to fear.

I'm a child of God, yes, I am.

Prayer:

Dear Abba Father, Thank You so much for sending Christ to redeem us so that we can be adopted into Your family, brothers and sisters in Christ and with Christ. Please give me clarity in that identity and value as I face my daily challenges and struggles. Help me always to remember that I am a child of God first and foremost. I am who You say I am. In Christ's name, Amen.

Questions:

1. Describe a time when you felt rejected or worthless.

2. How can you view that situation differently, knowing your true identity as a believer?

3. How can knowing you are an adopted child of God, change the way you live today and in the future?

4. How can Ephesians 2:10 build on the message of your identity in Christ?

Can I Ask You A Personal Question?
by Dr. Roy E. Lucas, Jr.

Will Rogers said, "I never met a man I didn't like." Tom Patterson embodies this motto with a Christian twist. Tom never meets a man he won't ask his favorite questions.

Without reservations, Tom posed his personal question to a waitress at a pizza restaurant in Harlan, Kentucky. Tom caught the waitress thinking about taking our drink orders. His personal question humbled me as I sat closed mouth and saying to myself, "Why didn't I ask her before Tom?" Having been with Tom as much as I have, I knew he was going to ask his question.

Tom asks everyone he meets, "Can I ask you a personal question?" From my observations, Tom receives almost 100 percent affirmative responses to his question. Tom asks this personal question intending to follow it with an eternal question, "Do you have a vital relationship with Jesus Christ?"

At a State Baptist Convention in Kentucky, Tom asked a security guard his question while hundreds of other ministers, pastors, college professors, college presidents, and state convention leaders passed the guard unnoticed. Tom posed his second question, "Do you have a vital relationship with Jesus Christ?" The security guard confessed faith in the Lord in the foyer of the convention hall.

While prayer-walking near his home in Barbourville, Kentucky, Tom approached an 84-year-old man and asked his questions. Days earlier, Tom had encountered a man strolling with his granddaughter at Walmart in the same city, and asked his questions. I have witnessed Tom pose his two questions across southern Kentucky, in Chicago, Illinois, in Tel Aviv, Israel, and even in Jerusalem. Tom doesn't always hear the person confess Christ as Lord and Savior, but Tom provides an opportunity with his questions. Tom obeys Christ's command in Matthew 28:19-20, "to go."

What Does Jesus Want Us to Know?

Jesus wants all believers to make disciples.

Go therefore and make disciples of all the nations, baptizing them in the name of the Father and of the Son and of the Holy Spirit, teaching them to observe all things that I have commanded you; and lo, I am with you always, even to the end of the age. Amen. (Matthew 28:19-20 NKJV)

The main verb of these verses is *make disciples* (NKJV) or *teach* (KJV). Jesus explains that disciples mature when three actions happen: going, baptizing, and teaching. The three actions build on one another. If no one is going, then no one will be baptized. If no one goes and no one is baptized, then no one teaches. Disobedience abounds when we fail to "go."

I used to teach the most accurate translation for "go" was, "as you go or when you go." I asserted all Christians are always going. And for the most part, we go all the time. We go to the grocery store, to the bank, to get gas, to school, to the post office, and so on.

However, reviewing this verse in personal study, I ran across a Greek Grammar textbook that taught me the error of my teaching.

I learned that while "Go" grammatically functions as a participle in the Greek text, an acceptable translation of the word is a command, like "make disciples." Thus, the translations that use, "Go," offer a proper translation. Therefore, as disciples of Jesus, we cannot wait for a convenient time to go to make disciples. Jesus intended His disciples to be proactive rather than passive. Thus I share, "Go and make disciples by baptizing and teaching them."

What Does Jesus Want Us to Do?

First, I know Jesus' command in Matthew 28:19-20 says to go, so I will go. I will go intending to seize every opportunity to share the Gospel.

Second, I know my motivation to go intensifies as I recall my life in sin before my conversion to follow Christ. Formerly sin mastered my life, and I served sin without care. Now, I am free to serve Jesus. He is my new Master. The Holy Spirit indwells me and influences my decisions and desires so I want to go.

Third, I know Jesus commanded me to go with the same love and compassion He possessed. Compassion overwhelmed Jesus when He regarded the people like sheep without a shepherd. He touched the leper, welcomed the Samaritans, embraced the diseased, encouraged the discouraged, showered grace upon the harlot, and fellowshipped with the sinner.

Last, I know Jesus *desires all men to be saved and to come to the knowledge of the truth* (1 Timothy 2:4 NKJV). Jesus instructed His disciples to go until every person has heard the life-changing truth of Jesus Christ's death, burial, and resurrection. I need to be about the Lord's business by listening for the call of the ages, and by going into the portion of the world where He has placed me or where He sends me. I could follow the example of a good friend of mine, and engage more people in conversation about Jesus.

Prayer:

Father, Help us to purposely "go." Move me to obedience to Your command to go and to make disciples. Help me to be motivated to go as my relationship with You deepens daily. Give me a heart for the lost that looks like Your heart. May I experience a measure of Your compassion for those who walk and live without a relationship with You. May I see the potential in individuals that my society would toss away just as You had eyes for the downtrodden and defeated. Open my spiritual ears to hear You and my physical mouth to ask others, "Can I ask you a personal question?" Amen.

Questions:

1. Jesus set a model for going. Scan any gospel and make a list of some of the places He visited. How did the people respond to Him?

2. Scan Acts. Make a list of some of the places where Peter and Paul traveled, to share the gospel. What do you think drove them to be so committed?

3. Why would we go to another city or state, or to a different country to share the gospel, if we do not share it where we "go" daily? What new habits might help us to share the gospel more regularly?

4. Would you consider your safety before the eternal salvation of another person? Why or why not?

5. How can we practice Romans 10:9-16 in our own sphere of influence?

The Power of Prayer
Introduction

In this section of *The Power to Make a Difference*, the authors take us behind the scenes of their public lives and share insights and encouragement on the blessings of prayer.

They help us to see prayer with fresh eyes as they compare the fluid rhythms of prayer to dancing, take us on a walking tour of everyday lives and prayer needs, share their deep praise of our glorious God, and show us the power, protection, and wonder of prayer.

They include practical tips on how we can remember others' prayer requests, on choosing the best time of day for prayer, and on how to make prayer a vital habit of daily life. They confirm that prayer is a precious privilege that taps into a treasure house of supply for our daily needs, and that presents solutions for our daily challenges. May these studies refresh your energy and enthusiasm to make the most of the awesome resource of prayer.

Ask, and you will receive, that your joy may be full.
(John 16:24 NKJV)

The Dance of Prayer
by Jonathan McDuffie

Sixth grade. Sweaty palms. A dimly lit gym and a poorly tied tie. It was my first middle school dance, and uncomfortable would be an understatement. While dancing appears to be the epitome of joy, more often than not, dancing sent shock waves of insecurity through my soul.

For many, prayer brings the same feelings of self-doubt. When asked to pray publicly, many feel the same tinges of fear. Even in private prayer, some of us worry we don't pray enough about the right subjects. We lose focus. Our prayer lacks direction, and we fall into the same awkward pattern of prayer.

Perhaps a new perspective will help. Just as music moves us to dance, God's Word stirs us to pray. Much like dancing, Scripture provides steps that give focus and direction to our prayers. Let the following verses guide you in prayer.

Up

Make a joyful shout to the LORD, all you lands!
Serve the LORD with gladness;
come before His presence with singing.
Know that the LORD, He is God.
(Psalm 100:1-3 NKJV®)

Our first step in the dance of prayer is UP. *The LORD, He is God*. When we consider the Greatest Commandment, when we remember the opening lines of the Lord's Prayer, our hearts are tuned to our number one priority in prayer—praising God. As we enter into prayer, there is no better beginning than to lift up words of praise.

Down

*If we confess our sins,
He is faithful and just to forgive us our sins
and to cleanse us from all unrighteousness.*
(1 John 1:9)

After lifting up our praise, we turn the focus of our prayers DOWN in confession and repentance. One of my close friends is a football team's physical trainer. He lives in the gym, and he looks like it. Any time I am with him, I am immediately aware of my own failure in fitness and physique. The same is often true in our relationship with God. After praising God for His majestic, wonderful qualities, we are painfully cognizant of our own shortcomings. Praise leads to prayers of confession.

Forward

*But we all, with unveiled face,
beholding as in a mirror the glory
of the Lord, are being transformed into the same image
from glory to glory, just as by the Spirit of the Lord.*
(2 Corinthians 3:18)

We've prayed prayers of praise. We've prayed prayers of confession. Now it's time to lift our downward gaze FORWARD. After repenting of our sins, it's time to turn our attention towards the present and the future, asking God to work in our lives to conform us into the image of His Son. I find that Scripture is often helpful at this stage. Praying through the Beatitudes or the Fruit of the Spirit gives even more focus to my prayers and curbs my sometimes selfish supplications towards a more God-honoring trajectory.

Right

> *Therefore I exhort first of all that supplications,*
> *prayers, intercessions,*
> *and giving of thanks be made for all men.*
> (1 Timothy 2:1)

After focusing our prayer on God and ourselves, we can now turn our attention to others, starting with our RIGHT-hand people. Paul challenges us to pray for other believers, and at this point, the list seems almost endless. Family, church family, small group members, pastors, missionaries, and our persecuted brothers and sisters. Some people simply let the Spirit lead. Some tend to have a more fixed prayer list. Others fluctuate between the two. Either way, our prayers must begin to move beyond ourselves to the greater family of God.

Left

> *But when He saw the multitudes,*
> *He was moved with compassion for them,*
> *because they were weary and scattered,*
> *like sheep having no shepherd.*
> (Matthew 9:36)

Finally, our last direction, those LEFT out of the kingdom. We all have people in our circles of influence who do not know Christ. We can't change their hearts, but Jesus can. Let us be faithful in lifting up the lost to our Lord.

Dancing has never been my strong suit. But if I've ever come close to enjoying dance, it's line dancing. There is something about the entire room moving together. No one stands out. No one is on their own. The mass moves together, in sync. That's the way I want my prayers to interact with God. I want my prayers to move with His Spirit to the rhythm of His words.

My dancing may always be awkward. But these steps have helped provide some much-needed direction in my prayer life, and I hope they will be of use to you as well.

Prayer:

Father, Would You give direction to my prayers? Would You direct my heart towards Your purposes and the people in my life who need a special touch from You? Amen.

Questions:

1. Do you use any favorite Bible verses to praise God? Do any songs inspire your praise of Him?

2. What does Romans 2:4 say about repentance?

3. How would you like God to work in your life currently?

4. Do you often make a particular request for the family of God?

5. Have you ever prayed Acts 26:18 for those who don't know God?

---

*All Scripture verses are taken from the NKJV.

Lord, Hear My Prayer
by Katherine Pasour

As I write this, I've just finished a telephone conversation with my daughter. She's on the way to the hospital. It's less than three weeks from her due date, but her blood pressure has skyrocketed and she's retaining fluid at a level to cause concern. At the close of our conversation, I lifted my eyes to heaven and prayed for my daughter and her baby girl.

Lord, hear my prayer.

For the past twenty-one years, while teaching at a Lutheran College, weekly Chapel on Wednesday mornings has always been a priority in my schedule. The Lutheran service is a little different from what I'm most familiar with (I'm a Methodist), but I still love the praise, worship, and peace I find from Chapel.

As part of the service, the campus Pastor often reads a series of individual prayer petitions and the people respond after each one with, "Lord, hear our prayer."

Something about all those voices in unison calling out to God, is both powerful and comforting. We feel that in our worship services, don't we? When we repeat the Lord's prayer, we feel His presence in our midst. As we lift our voices in songs of praise, we feel the sheer joy of praising our Father. We feel His strength and power in our group Bible studies, when we call on our prayer warriors, and when we hold hands and pray around our dinner table.

Group prayer is powerful, but God hears our individual prayers too. They are powerful as well.

LORD, hear my prayer, listen to my cry for mercy; in your faithfulness and righteousness come to my relief (Psalm 143:1 NIV®).

One crisp fall day, when my son was a college student, he hurried outside to drive to class (he usually was on the verge of being late). He rushed back in …

"Mom! Someone got into my car last night!"

"What? Any damage? Anything missing?"

He scuffed his shoe and looked down. "Uh … I think I forgot to lock it. There's no damage to the car. They took my watch and some money I had on the console …" His guilty gaze met mine, "And, they took my backpack."

My heart sank. "Your books?"

He nodded. "What will I do?"

His books had been exceptionally expensive that semester. Scholarships covered tuition, but we bought books out of pocket. It would take weeks to reorder (this was before the days of Amazon).

"I can't believe I didn't lock my car!" He paced the tiny kitchen.

"You need to go on to class. Explain why you're late."

"But, what about the books?" He stopped walking and spread his hands. "I've got an exam on Friday!"

I sat at the kitchen table and rested my forehead in my hands. "I don't know."

He touched my shoulder. "I'm sorry, Mom."

I patted his hand. "Better get to class. You're already late."

"I love you." He rushed out the door.

I prayed. I didn't know what else to do. I prayed that whoever took my son's books would return them.

Hear my prayer, LORD; listen to my cry for mercy. When I am in distress, I call to you, because you answer me (Psalm 86:6-7).

That night we found my son's backpack beside the dumpster at the apartment complex. All his books were inside—undamaged.

If you believe, you will receive whatever you ask for in prayer (Matthew 21:22).

I confess, at the time, I wasn't sure that I believed God would return my son's books. It seemed such a small thing for God to be concerned about. But I was desperate. I prayed, and God was merciful.

The issue in regard to my son's college books was money (or lack of it to buy new books).

But, now? My daughter and her unborn baby are in danger.

But our God is the God of love. He cares for us in all circumstances.

Our God is with us.

Yes, my soul, find rest in God; my hope comes from him. Truly he is my rock and my salvation; he is my fortress, I will not be shaken (Psalm 62:5-6).

Lord, hear my prayer.

> *Rejoice in the Lord always. I will say it again: Rejoice! ...*
> *Do not be anxious about anything, but in every situation,*
> *by prayer and petition, with thanksgiving,*
> *present your requests to God.*
> *And the peace of God which transcends all understanding,*
> *will guard your hearts and your minds in Christ Jesus.*
> (Philippians 4:4-7)

Prayer:

Father, We are so thankful for Your faithfulness in hearing our prayers. When we are fearful and cry out to You—You hear our prayer. When we have doubts and waver in our own faithfulness, You remain faithful and ever trustworthy. When our hope falters, You remain strong and support us on our journey. Thank You, gracious Lord, for Your great love for us, for always listening when we cry out to You.

Questions:

1. How does it affect you when God answers your specific prayers?

2. In Psalm 143:1, what attributes of God encourage us to pray to Him?

3. What reason does Psalm 86:6-7 give us to go to God when we are distressed?

4. What promise does Jesus give us in Matthew 21:22?

5. What four truths in Psalm 62:5-6 help us to find rest in God?

6. What antidote to worry is prescribed in Philippians 4:4? In v.7, what will the peace of God do?

---

*All Scripture verses are taken from the NIV.

Eight Strategies for Remembering Prayer Requests
by Jeannie Waters

My Indy 500 day blew past like Dale Earnhardt. I looked at the clock. "Oh, no! It's 3:00. I completely missed my daughter's test time."

I'd always promised to pray for her success on final exams. This time, however, I neglected to fulfill this important responsibility.

Have you ever promised to pray for someone's broken heart or surgery or job interview and then realized later that you'd forgotten? We mean well, but our memories sometimes fail.

In my teen years, I often voiced prayer needs to a mentor. She would respond, "Let's pray now. I don't want to forget." Her statements emphasized the responsibility of receiving a request and the importance of lifting it to our heavenly Father.

The Bible teaches, "Devote yourselves to prayer, keeping alert in it with an attitude of thanksgiving" (Colossians 4:2 NASB®). Commending fervent prayer, Paul wrote, "Epaphras … sends you his greetings, always laboring earnestly for you in his prayers, that you may stand perfect and fully assured in all the will of God" (Colossians 4:12).

Do you use memory aides or organizational techniques for important responsibilities like prayer? Methods for remembering the needs we notice can help us honor the privilege of communicating with God on behalf of others.

I hope you can use or adapt one of the following strategies.

1. Listen attentively to requests.

Listen carefully while establishing eye contact, and ask an appropriate question or repeat the focus to enhance your memory. When the ladies in my email prayer group read a request, they often ask a clarifying question and inquire later about results. This practice encourages believers and reflects the love of Christ to those who have not yet met Him.

2. Seek God's help.

Ask the Father to remind you of requests and to lead you to an applicable Bible verse to use as a prayer springboard. On busy days, we sometimes hear a soft whisper in our minds and hearts reminding us of the need to pray.

3. Organize an index card file.

Use a simple file box with index cards and tabs to categorize requests and provide space for recording answers. Some requests are long-term and may require multiple cards. When I used this method of memory prompts, I enjoyed reviewing the cards in the "Answered Prayer" section which demonstrated God's faithfulness.

4. Create a prayer journal or notebook.

A small loose-leaf binder can house dividers labeled with days of the week or categories like family, neighbors, church, missionaries, urgent, and government leaders. I am currently using this system with a tab for each day. Before the first divider, I added sheets labeled "Week of ___" to which I add Monday's date and requests specific to that week.

5. Use sticky notes.

For urgent situations or daily reminders, affix colorful sticky notes to the refrigerator, a mirror, computer, key chain, or steering wheel. A friend once wrote a note about praying for our family's concern and placed it on his office shelves. Each time he sat at his desk, he saw the reminder and prayed. Assurance that our need was being lifted to the Lord calmed our hearts.

6. Set a timer or phone reminder.

This practice averts the thought, "I'm busy now. I'll pray later." With phone reminders, a quickly typed label can jog our memory and sharpen our focus. Today, while concentrating on writing, I'm praying for a friend's health as she travels with airline delays and for family members on a lengthy road trip. While it's unlikely I will forget these loved ones, my phone alarm cues me to continue prayer support throughout the day.

7. Design a bookmark.

Record a long-term request on a bookmark. Add an appropriate verse and insert it into a book you're currently reading. You could write the same verse on an additional bookmark and mail it to the person you're praying for with an encouraging note.

8. Construct a small table tent.

Write prayer reminders on stiff paper, fold tent-style, and place on the coffee table or beside your spot at the dinner table. Change the location from time to time to ensure the tent catches your eye.

When the minutes in your day fly by with racecar speed, perhaps using one of these strategies will bring prayer requests to mind. Although communication with God requires no system, reminders can keep us on track. Paul said, "We give thanks to God, the Father of our Lord Jesus Christ, praying always for you" (Colossians 1:3). What a worthy goal for us!

Prayer:

Heavenly Father, You are Almighty God and yet You welcome us to Your throne of grace as beloved children. Thank You for the privilege of prayer. Tender our hearts to notice the needs of others and help us remember to lift those needs to You. In Jesus' name we pray, Amen.

Questions:

1. Which of the eight strategies above do you think would work best for you?

2. Do you regularly use any Bible verses as a springboard for prayer?

3. If you use sticky notes to remind you to pray, where do you put yours?

4. Do you have other ways to remember prayer requests?

---

*All Scripture verses are taken from the NASB.

The Slow Work of God
by Becky Hitchcock

On the modest plot in South Georgia where I live, work, and play, I like things slow. It's reflected in my word choices and speech patterns. Slow is my standard operating procedure. I don't like to be rushed. And rushing others is rude so I try not to do it.

A few years ago, I came across these words: "Above all," the author quoted Pierre Teilhard de Chardin, "trust in the slow work of God."[1]

I'm not familiar with the late Chardin, but I like the quote. It reminds me of my notebook. I'm quite fond of my little notebook. A thoughtful friend gave it to me. It's useful in my times of being still and knowing that God is God and I am not. These times of stillness are based on Psalm 46:10.

In the measure of an hour that turns into a day that soon turns into a decade, a multitude of prayers crosses my lips. Many are answered with great joy. So many that I always fall asleep before I'm done counting them. Truly, God is good. He has compassion on all that belongs to Him (Psalm 145:9).

However, one very BIG request, a fervent desire, has yet to be. It stays continually on my mind, heart, and lips. It's ever before me. My prayer—what I want so much to see—is in keeping with Scripture. When the answer comes to pass, many broken people will be healed. Great glory will be given to God. Unspeakable joy will peal throughout the small corner of my modest plot. That joy would then reach to the four corners of the globe.

So the waiting is difficult. It's hard to understand the delay. Especially when it seems with each passing day, the answer is farther from my grasp. Waiting for such an answer makes me rethink my stance on liking things slow. I want the answer right now. And I find myself anxious, weary, and impatient even though I don't want to be.

Yet in my times of being still, I find God is always present. Even though He takes His own sweet time in bringing things to pass, He is so trustworthy. He is the Creator of time. He is the Master of time. He's not limited to the passage of time in the way that I understand it. He never runs late, so any attempt to rush Him is useless.

The writer of Ecclesiastes tells me in Chapter 3 that there is a season for everything. Everything has its own time. I read in verse 11 (NIV®):

He has made everything beautiful in its time. He has also set eternity in the human heart; yet no one can fathom what God has done from beginning to end.

In Deuteronomy 29:29, I find:

The secret things belong to the LORD our God, but the things revealed belong to us and to our children forever, that we may follow all the words of this law.

My angst is eased when I ponder these words. I'm reminded that time is a matter of eternity. Even though God has put eternity in our hearts, the timing of eternity is all God's doing. His business, so to speak. And there are some things—secret things—that belong to Him alone. When my prayer will be answered must be a secret thing. It is not for me to fathom. It's not for me to grasp.

But the things He has shown me, the things He has revealed, like His Word that became flesh and is so full of grace and truth

(John 1:14) and those already answered prayers that are too numerous to count. I can fathom these. They are mine to grasp right now.

I want to enjoy them. I want to follow them. I want to share them with my children and with those who struggle with their own unanswered prayers. Many are waiting, just like me, for an answer to a prayer that stays continually on their minds, hearts, and lips. In this life, waiting is like another standard operating procedure.

And so, in my being still times, I will think on these things. I will remember that God is God and I am not. I will ponder the Chardin quote. I will keep my notebook handy. And I will not rush God because rushing is rude.

So maybe, I *am* learning to trust in the slow work of God.

Prayer:

Gracious God, Thank You for hearing my prayers. There are so many crossing my lips and staying on my heart and mind. Grant me a greater sense of You. Help me grasp the prayers You have already answered. Help me to be grateful. Forgive my futile attempts to rush You. Teach me to trust You with the secret things that are not yet revealed. For truly, there has never been a more caring God than You. In Jesus' name, Amen.

Questions:

1. Is your standard operating procedure slow or brisk?

2. If you are asking God to do something and the pace of His work seems to be slow, what encourages you to keep asking and to keep trusting?

3. What eternal benefits touch your life now, that are the result of "the slow work of God"?

4. *Be still and know that I am God* (Psalm 46:10). Why do you think being still is related to knowing God?

---

*All Scripture verses are taken from the NIV.
1. Pierre Teilhard de Chardin, https://www.goodreads.com/quotes/554784-above-all-trust-in-the-slow-work-of-god-we.

Save Your Amen
by J. D. Wininger

After eighteen difficult hours of dealing with a client, my blessing came after a three-hour nap in my San Antonio hotel room. I simply refer to it as "saving my Amen."

My clients were paying me to lead them through a task that they clearly did not want to do. It was like trying to get your children to eat vegetables that they don't like. It was a challenge!

Well, I woke up and immediately began doing what I always try and do—thanking God for the day ahead of me. As usual, it went along the lines of, *"Father, thank You for giving me another day on this Earth. Thank You for keeping me and my family safe, and please help me to do something this day that glorifies You."*

Like probably every other Christian in the world, I ask God to be patient with me, to forgive my failures, and I invite His Holy Spirit to remain close in my heart and help guide me through the day. Of course, I always pray for blessings for my wife Diane, my family, my church, and my great friends. And like most of us, I end my prayers with, *"In Jesus' name I pray, Amen."*

Well, that particular morning, God did not want me to end my prayer. He told me, in that small, quiet voice I hear when He gives me that "heart hug": *"Why did you stop? You're not done yet."* So, like the obsessive compulsive I am, I said, *"Huh?,"* and started running through my mental list of people and things to pray about. He told me again, *"You're not done yet."* This time He added: *"Go read Chapter 5 of First Thessalonians."*

Well, what do you do when God tells you to do something? You betcha, you go find that Gideon's Bible in the hotel room and you read 1 Thessalonians Chapter 5. Sure enough, I started reading and I'm thinking to myself, *"Here's Paul advising us how to spend the day walking with the Lord."* Then about in the middle of my reading, it hit me in verse 17 (NKJV), "Pray without ceasing."

That's when I felt my "heart hug" get tighter as I had tears by this time, and I heard, *"Why say Amen? Why stop?"* Of course, I responded with, *"Cause that's how you end prayers, Father."* You see *Amen* is how we close our prayers, it's akin to saying, *"Let Your will be done, God."* To which I then heard, *"Exactly! You end, and then you go out and become of this world. That's not what I want you to be."*

I realized that when I am praying, I am on my very best behavior. I don't curse under my breath, I seldom call that person I think is an idiot an idiot, and I try my best to be the person that I believe God wants me to be. What God chose to reveal to me at 4 a.m. there in a hotel room in San Antonio, Texas was that He expected me to be that person—to be that prayerful, thoughtful, submitting person who asks for guidance, forgiveness, and patience—all the time; not just when I was praying and worshipping Him.

So, I've adopted a tactic that has blessed me more than I could have ever imagined. Rather than doing my normal routine of praying in the morning when I awake, and then praying before meals and ending my day with a prayer as I lie in bed; I now pray throughout the day and *"Save My Amen"* for the end of the day, just before I close my eyes and drift off to sleep. And the next morning, I start again.

Prayer:

Father, I thank You for the wonderful gift of being able to come and speak with You throughout my day. When the pressures and stresses of this world begin to weigh me down, I can call out to You with a request for peace. When I feel troubled by something

I've said or done, or when something said or done to me brings pain, I can prayerfully crawl into Your lap, Abba, and be soothed by Your endless grace. Father God, I pray that all who read this can find and share that same loving relationship with You throughout their days. In Jesus' precious name I pray.

Questions:

1. How might keeping your dialog with God open throughout your day benefit you? Will it bring you more peace, more comfort, more self-control?

2. Often sitting back, closing your eyes, and meditating for just a few moments can help restore your peace. Wouldn't taking a rest in God's presence through a short, silent prayer invite Him to come and sit with you?

3. Do you always remember to ask God for guidance to understand or prepare a response to something said? Do you silently pray for the Holy Spirit's guidance before you speak? That's prayer.

Listening for God's Voice
by Katy Kauffman

The Power of God's Voice

A song glided over the mountains and slipped through the window of my hotel room, or so I thought. As I woke up in one of my favorite places on earth, the Blue Ridge Mountains, I strained to hear the melody of some faint sound. *Where is that coming from? Can the mountains really sing?*

I turned on the light and almost decided the mountain tops possessed some magical quality. And then I discovered it. The new alarm app on my tablet was quietly urging me to wake up. The volume was turned down so low I didn't even realize it was speaking to me.

The Power of God's Volume

There have been times in my life that I wanted God to blare an answer to my question or trumpet the timing of His plan. But I've discovered that it's the quiet moments that take His soft reply and sear His answer on my heart. He doesn't need to shout. He simply needs to whisper. Do we realize He is speaking to us?

God's choice method of communication to the mighty prophet Elijah was not a show of overwhelming strength. God didn't appear to him in a great wind, a tumultuous earthquake, or a raging fire. *A still small voice* (1 Kings 19:12 NKJV®) glided over the mountain to Elijah's hiding place in the cave. God reassured him that seven thousand people were still faithful to the one true God in a land ruled by an idolatrous king and queen. God also gave him his next assignment—to find Elisha, his future apprentice. Elijah wouldn't have to continue his ministry alone. God's comforting words enabled him to keep moving forward with His plan, enabling Elijah to overcome fear with the promises of God and faith in the One who gave them.

The Power of God's Word

> *Your ears shall hear a word*
> *behind you, saying,*
> *"This is the way, walk in it,"*
> *whenever you turn*
> *to the right hand or*
> *whenever you turn to the left.*
> (Isaiah 30:21)

You shall hear a word … just a *word*. A simple word from God can make all the difference in the trajectory of our lives and the strength of our hearts. What word do you need to hear from Him today?

I have loved you with an everlasting love (Jeremiah 31:3).

You are mine (Isaiah 43:1).

I am with you always (Matthew 28:20).

Go and sin no more (John 8:11).

With God all things are possible (Mark 10:27).

God knows when we need comfort and strength, and He also knows when we need a specific word of direction. He gives it to us at just the right time. If we're listening. A close relationship with God in which we constantly depend on Him and ask Him for guidance, turns anxiety into peace and ignorance into wisdom. When we lack wisdom, we can ask God for help and He will give it (James 1:5) in just the right way at just the right time.

Anxiety churned within me. More than once. I didn't know what to do, and I didn't want to do the wrong thing. I wanted to use my brain and make an informed decision, but more than anything, I wanted God path's, not my own. So I asked Him—about a relationship, about a job opportunity, for comfort, to intervene. He answered.

Sometimes I questioned whether the answer came from my heart or God's. But asking a certain question usually helps me to know whether the source of the answer is God or not. "Father, if You were to bind all other voices and I were to hear only from You and do Your will, what is Your will about …?" This question usually yields an answer before I even finish saying it. Hearing from God brings peace to our hearts, direction for our lives, and His best path for our today and tomorrow. Are our hearts and minds willing to receive His answer?

The Power of an Open Heart and Mind

God is speaking—are we willing to listen? Pride says, "I can handle it." Humility says, "I will seek God's guidance." Anxiety says, "I don't know how this is going to turn out and I need to know." Peace says, "I will seek God's will about this and rest in His answer." Are we willing to set aside our own wisdom and fears to listen for God's guidance?

Building a history with God makes us more and more willing to listen for His voice. We know He speaks the truth and gives perfect direction. He can see what we can't, and He knows how a situation will turn out. He loves us without flaw or hindrance, perfectly, and can do anything He wants. When we have seen Him act on our behalf, it helps us to trust Him for next time. So trust. Ask Him for what you need. Expect an answer. God loves His children and wants to lead us, comfort us, and strengthen us.

How have you seen God turn anxiety into peace and desperation into wisdom? Hold on to those moments when the voice of God intervened in your life, and keep seeking Him. His voice will be our constant guide until we arrive in heaven, and with

His help and direction we will accomplish His will for us on this earth.

Prayer:

Dear Father, Quiet my heart that I may hear the "word" You want to speak to me. Remove any anxiety and pride so I can hear You clearly. Thank You in advance for guiding me, and thank You that Your love is so great that You take the time to speak to each of Your children. Help us to take enough time to listen. In Jesus' name, Amen.

Questions:

1. Is there a particular way that you ask God for direction, and you can be sure it's His voice and not your own?

2. What evidence has God given you, that taking time to listen to His voice is worth the time spent?

3. What can hinder us from hearing God clearly?

4. How can we deal with those hindrances?

5. Of the five verses listed under the heading, "The Power of God's Word," which "word" from God do you need the most today?

6. Think of a friend or family member who needs to hear from God. Pray for them a verse of Scripture that would help them right now.

---

*All Scripture verses are taken from the NKJV.

Prayerwalking: Praying with Compassion
by Krystal Weeks

When [Jesus] saw the multitudes, He was moved with compassion for them, because they were weary and scattered, like sheep having no shepherd. Then He said to His disciples, "The harvest truly is plentiful, but the laborers are few. Therefore pray the Lord of the harvest to send out laborers into His harvest." (Matthew 9:36-38 NKJV)

We are those laborers who can pray and go. One way that we can do both, is prayerwalking.

Prayerwalking is praying with compassion for others while you are in their surroundings, while you are walking where they walk and live. It carries God's stamp of approval, and it is a special way that we can feel His presence with us as we become His hands and feet in the world.

J. Chris Schofield states in his booklet *Prayerwalking Made Simple*, "On-site prayer helps us gain a proper God-sized perspective on people and their individual struggles. We see the reality of people in their lostness—the hopeless, helpless, bound and blinded condition of those separated from Christ."[1] It's humbling to think God desires to communicate and fellowship with us through prayer, and the Holy Spirit leads us as we present the hope of Christ to our tormented world.

The first time I prayerwalked, we prayed aloud with our eyes open looking at passing cars, people walking down the street, everything related to people and their lives. We even prayed for businesses. We stood on the sidewalk outside an adult entertainment store and prayed it would close down.

We also talked to myriad groups of people in Hispanic stores, on the street, or in their cars. We prayed with people who were alcoholics, homeless and defeated, as well as people who were working or out for a walk. When we were walking through apartments close to a university, I spoke to a young Asian, Oscar, who was standing in his doorway. I asked him if I could show him the EvangeCube. After seeing the pictures of the life of Christ, he prayed and accepted Christ as his Savior. My soul was filled with gratitude for this movement of the Holy Spirit in his life. Listening as other team members spoke to individuals about Christ's love caused my heart to overflow with joy realizing the power of intercessory prayer.

The last time I went prayerwalking, we walked around an apartment complex. We walked and prayed as we looked at the buildings, cars, even people on their balconies. We prayed for those who had handicap stickers, or items in their cars that gave us a window to their stress-filled lives. One girl was washing her car, and we asked her how we could pray for her. She did not grasp what we were saying at first, but as we continued to talk, she asked us to pray for her boyfriend who was flying that day.

Next we saw a father and son who were putting their dirt bikes on a trailer. The father asked us to pray for his son's friends who have cancer. As we proceeded through the area, we met a young woman out for a walk. She said she deals with homicide cases, and the night before had been a "rough night." I told her I pray for those in Harm's Way at my church, and I would pray for her by name and for the rest of her team.

Our last contact was with a young man who said he had just moved to our city. After he warmed up to our offer to pray for him, he told us his family members were believers. He asked us to pray for them and for him as he started his new job. We told him about churches in the area, and he said we made his day. He definitely made our day too.

Prayerwalking with Christ—no better place to be—doing His work and experiencing His powerful presence in and through our lives. That is how our world is impacted with the gospel.[2] Prayerwalking for me has been truly an exhilarating experience and has given me confirmation that I am fulfilling God's purpose in my life.

So if you have not been prayerwalking yet, join God as He works, feel His presence through your praying, and shout the victory for what you will see Him accomplish through your surrender.

Prayer:

Dear God, Give us a heart of love for the hurting and the lost that we see around us. Open our eyes to opportunities to prayerwalk, even if it is just in our neighborhood. Remind us we can make a difference through our surrender and show of compassion for those who are filled with hopelessness. Help us, Lord, to pray without ceasing so we may bear fruit for Your kingdom.

Questions:

1. Does the author's description of what she saw as she went prayerwalking, broaden your perspective of how to pray for others?

2. What do these verses say about prayer?
    a. Luke 18:1
    b. Luke 10:2
    c. Colossians 1:9-10
    d. Colossians 4:2-3a

3. What is Christ sending us to do in Acts 26:16b-18?

4. What reminder does Ephesians 3:20 give us, that encourages us to pray?

1. J. Chris Schofield, *Prayerwalking Made Simple* (Cary, North Carolina: Baptist State Convention of North Carolina, 2018), 8.
2. Ibid., 9.

White-Knuckled Urgency: The Prayer of Faith
by Mary Holloman

"Dear God, gank You for cars and dump trucks and street sweepers. And most of all, gank You for Jesus, Your Son, who died for our sins. Amen."

Before "amen" even finished rolling off his tongue, my three-year-old firecracker began shoveling food into his mouth much like the dump trucks—which he so reverently lifted up in prayer—might slide mounds of dirt into a bottomless pit. I clenched my teeth to bite back the laughter that threatened to spill over. When my son paused from filling his hollow legs with pasta, he took a breath and launched into an epic reenactment of his day.

My son is many things, but apathetic is not one of them. I've never seen him do anything halfway. There is a sense of urgency in every task. When he builds with LEGO® bricks, his face remains inches from each piece, concentration etched into the soft lines of his furrowed brow. When he plays outside, there's no sauntering or meandering. Each task is completed at a dead run, usually accompanied by an imagined high speed car chase. When he tells stories, he's breathless, the excitement of sharing his thoughts almost more exhilarating than the events themselves.

And when he prays, his knuckles turn white as he clasps his hands, his eyes turn to slits (as close to closed as his antsy little body can manage) and he "ganks" God for whatever his heart has taken the most joy in that day.

Every task—every prayer—is done earnestly.

My tendency is to look at my son's enthusiasm for everyday tasks with a hint of cynicism. I'm not nearly as excited about washing dishes or paying bills or grocery shopping as my son is about the daily mundane. I don't operate with the same sense of urgency. This is partially due to necessity. If I sprinted through the grocery store and slam-dunked pieces of fruit and boxes of cereal into my cart at breakneck speed, I'd probably get detained by store security.

But if I'm honest, this cynicism is also due in part to an undercurrent of unbelief.

Rather than write off my little man's sense of urgency as naive, I've felt the Holy Spirit whispering to me through my son's simple faith. Scripture commands followers of Jesus to pray with an intensity that reflects a trust in Him above all else. Earnest prayer is not just a matter of "going through the motions." It is symptomatic of a heart that believes God hears me, loves me, and will respond to me in accordance with His will.

In the book of Luke, I was startled by one particular phrase in the parable of the persistent widow: "And will not God give justice to his elect, *who cry to him day and night*?" (Luke 18:7 ESV, emphasis mine).

A wave of conviction swept over me as the truth of this Scripture settled in. I'd always acknowledged the persistence of the widow, but never truly identified *with* her. She was the one who needed help, and needed it desperately—not me.

Yet here I saw the true reality: Not only am I the widow in desperate need of justice, but God is the righteous Judge who desires to give me the things I ask for according to His will. But here is the key: God gives to those who *cry to Him day and night*.

God responds to those who pray continually, without ceasing, with a thankful heart, and in all circumstances. To those who cry out in desperation, with complete and total dependence on the Father.

My three-year-old thanks God for every piece of joy in his life and asks Him for the simplest things because he knows and believes that God is the one who can and will answer. His faith is simple and pure—it's all he knows—and this leads him to pray with a white-knuckled-and-eyes-shut-tight kind of urgency.

When was the last time I hit my knees with this same degree of intense faith?

Because of Christ, I can approach the throne of grace with confidence, knowing that my heavenly Father hears me. Because of Christ, I can bring before God even the details of the daily mundane, knowing that He is sovereign over every moment. And because of Christ, I can cry to Him day and night, knowing that the one true God is the only one deserving of my undivided, wholehearted devotion and allegiance.

May my knees remain on the floor and my knuckles remain white. May the posture of my prayer reflect the posture of my heart. And may my faith stay childlike and my belief unbroken.

Prayer:

Father, What a privilege to come to You daily with all my fears, anxieties, praises, and joys. It's so easy for me to go through the motions of prayer without truly submitting to You in dependence and surrender. Lord, I need You every moment, every hour. Thank You for Your unconditional love and patience. Please help me to practice a growing faith in my prayer life.

Questions:

1. What in these verses encourages you to pray?
    a. James 5:16
    b. Psalm 34:15

    c. Psalm 145:18-19
    d. Matthew 7:7-8
    e. Matthew 21:22

2. From an above paragraph: "God responds to those who pray continually, without ceasing, with a thankful heart, and in all circumstances. To those who cry out in desperation, with complete and total dependence on the Father."

Which part of this do you think is the most difficult?

3. What does Hebrews 4:16 say about "the throne of grace"?

Search My Heart with Your Holiness
by Karen Fulgham

Search me, O God, and know my heart;
try me, and know my anxieties;
and see if there is any wicked way in me,
and lead me in the way everlasting.
(Psalm 139:23-24 NKJV)

Dear Lord,

Search my heart with Your holiness, Your Spirit within me.

Lead my heart to Your Holy will. Let me not fall to the deception of the nature within. My heart belongs to You, I give it this day and every day to Your holy purpose. Please test and try my heart so that the one who devours will not be able to get a foothold in my inner being or in my life.

As I read and study the Holy Word, the Scripture, divide my conscience toward holy truth. Let me not be deceived by cunning arguments, caught in the current grasp of the enemy. Free my mind, Lord, from any deceptive reasoning.

The Lord is my Shepherd, I will follow His voice. Help me to hear what You say, so that I know the Way. These feet are Yours, fitted with the readiness of the gospel that brings peace to the heart of all humanity who have the will to believe it.

Your righteousness guards my heart position, the place I find as home, the place of my hope, the place I rest. I am counted as Yours, You have named me with salvation, Your name is on my head. Faith in You, O Lord, guards me from penetrating piercings of misguides and deception coming toward me in fine sounding words, rationalized thoughts, cunning arguments, and natural desires. Faith in You, O Lord, stands me upright in the face of discouragement, failings, deception, persecution, rejection, and losses.

Grief is not wasted, but a transforming fire. Let it be as it is; my faith will remain in You.

Thank You, Lord, for wholeness and completeness within my core. This is who You have called me to be, in Spirit, living now in Your presence, in this day, living a holy purpose, for the sake of the name of Jesus Christ, the Savior of all mankind, saved from separation from Holy God which was caused by original sin in the beginning. Though this inherited sin state seeks after me, naturally desiring to consume me, Jesus freed me from its power to condemn me. My allegiance is now to Him!

The Holy Spirit that He sent, counsels and guides me to live in freedom today and each day given, be it clouded with worry or cleared by joy. I am blessed with holy privilege I did not earn, to live in this age of grace.

Thank You, my Lord, for loving this much, freeing so many, giving life, giving a burning hope, a fire fueling the lamp of this journey. In Jesus' name I pray, Amen!

Questions:

1. According to the paragraphs, which of our actions and commitments to God help us to live in the freedom and holiness that He has for us?

2. Many things are named that God does to help us live for Him. Which four are your favorites?

God's Well of Grace
by Billie Corley

While gathering the sticks, she breathed out a sigh,
The land had become barren and extremely dry.
A handful of meal and a little oil were all that remained
Despairingly she wondered if life would ever be the same.
Her hopes depleted, she had done what she could
But now the future looked bleak from where she stood.
As she was thinking about their last meal,
The startling request for water was surreal …
"And, while you're at it would you also bring me a cake?"
To which she replied, "I'm sorry, but you're too late.
It's not that I'm greedy and don't want to share
I have only enough and nothing to spare."
The man gently encouraged her to prepare for him first
And promised she'd never go hungry nor thirst.
With a trembling heart she granted his request,
All the while wondering if his promises were amiss.
After sharing her last meal, she walked back in a daze
But when she looked into the barrel, she was amazed!
All logic and reasoning testified she'd find it empty.
But just like the man of God said, there was plenty!
Day after day, through the parched desolate years
God's faithfulness to provide quenched all of her fears.
So, today my friend, be of good courage and choose to believe
The God of Creation will abundantly provide your every need.
No matter your circumstance, God's resources are always greater
Be assured He'll supply in abundance, yes, even now and later!

God is more than enough, and He "is able to do exceedingly abundantly above all that we ask or think" (Ephesians 3:20 NKJV').

This great promise is exemplified in the life of a widow who was struggling to survive during a time of drought. The dry earth prevented her from growing crops, and she had no other means of support. With no hope of survival, she made preparations to bake a cake using the last bit of oil and a handful of meal, and after that, she and her son would die. As she was gathering two sticks for fuel, God showed up through the prophet Elijah and miraculously provided food until the day He sent rain on the earth (1 Kings 17:14).

The asking and receiving concept is illustrated throughout Scripture. Yet, in the context of 1 Kings Chapter 17, petitioning God's help isn't mentioned until verse twenty. Nonetheless, valuable truths regarding prayer can be gleaned from Elijah and the widow's experience. How do these Scriptures authenticate that God is ready and willing to meet our every need?

First of all, we can delight in the fact that God is always one step ahead. There are times when God leads us to the solution even before we petition His help. Prayer is not meant to inform Him of that which He already knows. Rather it is a path to where He patiently listens to the cry of His people. In Matthew 6:8, Jesus taught the disciples, "Your Father knows the things you have need of before you ask Him."

We can also take heart that God is available 24/7 and is only a prayer away. We never have to panic in times of distress. Notice the first thing Elijah did when the widow's lifeless boy was placed in his arms, "he cried out to the LORD" (1 Kings 17:20). Satan taunts our prayer efforts by attempting to deceive us that "prayer doesn't do any good." But God's Word says, "Call upon Me in the day of trouble; I will deliver you, and you shall glorify Me" (Psalms 50:15).

We can rest knowing that God honors honesty. Sometimes we may be tempted to not express our true feelings before the Lord.

Elijah boldly opened the door to God's presence by not hiding his anguish. He poured out his fears before making his request to God (1 Kings 17:20-21). Psalms 142:2 encourages us to pour (spill out) our anxiety before God in times of trouble.

Finally, it's comforting to recognize how God uses answered prayer to fortify our faith. What was the widow's reaction to her son's illness? "O man of God ... Have you come to me to bring my sin to remembrance, and to kill my son?" (1 Kings 17:18). We have the choice to let our fears take charge or to recall God's faithfulness. His faithfulness encourages us to take our supplications before the Lord. Notice that God heard Elijah's voice "and the soul of the child came back to him, and he revived" (1 Kings 17:22). Many times we're devastated by our circumstances. We will do well to remember, our trials are just another opportunity for God to demonstrate His supreme power over and through our situation.

What about you? Are you in the midst of great testing and trouble? Are you parched and need to be filled with hope? Are life's pressures dehydrating your spirit? Remember, divine help is readily available. Psalm 102:17 assures us God will "regard the prayer of the destitute, and shall not despise their prayer." Yes, even when we don't have the stamina to call out to Him. So why don't you pull up to God's table, sit awhile, and drink freely from His Well of Grace which never runs dry. When your cup is empty, be sure and ask for a refill. They're unlimited.

Prayer:

Lord, How often our needs go unfulfilled because we fail to ask. Please forgive us for looking everywhere else but to Your throne of grace in our time of need. We thank You that no matter the size of our need, You're able to provide exceedingly and abundantly above all we ask or think. Thank You, Father, for making a way to make our needs known. We humbly bow before You with thankful hearts. In Jesus' holy name we pray. Amen.

Questions:

1. Has God ever "showed up" and provided for your needs when you despaired of having any help?

2. What does Philippians 4:19 say about our needs? Do you think that was demonstrated in the widow's situation?

3. What four truths in this study encourage us that God will meet our needs, and that it is wise to take the opportunity to pray to Him?

---

*All Scripture verses are taken from the NKJV.

Conclusion: Home

What does "home" mean to you? How grateful are you to have a home with people you love and who love you? What difference does your home and family make in your daily life and well-being? In the following short story, the difference was dramatic to a young woman's heart that longed to go home.

In this conclusion to *The Power to Make a Difference*, read the story and answer the questions at the end. They are based on the four topics of the book—The Power of Words, The Power of Doing, The Power of Knowing, and The Power of Prayer.

Home
by Lori Altebaumer

Home. The one place when you go there, they have to let you in.

Only not mine. That's why I stand across the street beneath the sycamore tree, staring through the night at the dim glow of lights puddling in a gray mist so heavy it soaks my skin. My hair plasters against my cheeks. I shiver.

The lights of home. They've been referred to as warm and welcoming. But not the lights of my home. Instead, the thick drapes are pulled shut, only the faintest of light escapes around their edges. The house has closed its eyes, refusing to see me.

I squint at the window on the second floor, the one where my parents' bedroom is, imagining I see movement, a subtle flutter of the window covering settling back into place. My mind playing tricks on me.

They aren't going to let me in. I know without even knocking. The daughter I had once been doesn't live there anymore. She doesn't live anywhere. And the person I am isn't welcomed there.

Do they ever think of me? Do they remember the sound of my voice or does a memory of something I said ever come to mind unexpectedly? Do they glance at the stairs and for just a moment expect to see me hurrying down, late for choir practice? Do they pass by my old room and out of habit peek inside, expecting to see me curled up in the window seat with some new book, lost to the world around me?

Or have they succeeded in erasing me from their memory? Does my birthday come as just another day, no different from any other?

Without seeing, I know nothing in the house has changed. The furniture will be in the same place it was the day I left five years ago. The same pictures on the wall and the same fake flowers sitting on the end table. The same hard hearts and tearless faces. Everything the same, except scrubbed clean of me. The memory of my presence in their lives like a scratch on the hardwood floor, buffed and polished until no trace of it remained. Rubbed out.

Change did not come easy in this house, if it ever came at all.

No. Home isn't the one place where they have to let you in.

The dark, seedy side of town—that is the place that will always let you in. The drug addicts and prostitutes, the depraved and destitute and desperate. There is always room for one more at the bottom.

I squeeze my clenched hand around the coat I hold closed above the broken zipper, but the chill making me shiver doesn't come from the cold, damp night.

The story of the prodigal son, restored to his full honor and position, his past seemingly swept away, comes to mind. It isn't that simple for the prodigal daughter. There are some things that can't be swept away.

"Are we going in, Mama?" The small hand clinging tightly to my cold fingers tugs on my arm.

I am thankful for the moisture already sticking to my face, so he doesn't see me cry.

"Not tonight, Son. Not tonight."

* * * * *

"There's a package been left for you," the volunteer at the front desk of the homeless shelter says when I return from taking Jonah to school the next morning. I've seen her before, but she's never spoken to me. She just watches me with Jonah in a way that tells me she doesn't approve. She wouldn't be the first person to tell me I am selfish for not wanting the best for my child. The best being giving him up for adoption. Maybe they're right. But I'm not trying to be selfish.

Maybe I was the night Jonah was conceived. Maybe then I was only thinking about me and what I wanted. But never again. Not since the moment I knew he existed inside me. And certainly not since the doctor at the free clinic told me Jonah is on the spectrum. That's the benign doctor way of saying Jonah is autistic. Mildly, and that's probably the only reason he hasn't been taken away from me. A homeless shelter is no place for a child who needs routine. Especially a quirky routine.

It rips my heart open to think of him being with someone who doesn't know he'll only sleep on his right side and can't stand the feel of anything fuzzy. Someone who doesn't understand his preoccupation with dinosaurs, that his pretending to be one is just a part of who he is. It takes a special kind of understanding to get a dinosaur dressed for school each day and put to bed at night. I have that special understanding.

I feel guilty for coming back here when I should be out there looking for a job. I don't know why this is where my feet brought me today. Maybe my heart just isn't ready to hear another no thank you. It isn't easy to find a job when you're a single mother whose place of residence is a homeless shelter.

"I'm not expecting anything," I tell her. She must have read the name wrong. I don't like the suspicious look she gives me—like just because I'm here I can't be trusted.

"I didn't make no mistake. I's here when the boy dropped it off and I can read." She hands the package to me, eyes narrowed. "You know you can't stay here if you get in any kind of trouble. They'll kick you back out on the street and take your child away."

I'd like to yell at her I'm well aware of what would happen, but yelling is frowned upon here, especially toward the volunteers, so I bite my tongue.

Getting into any kind of trouble isn't in my plans. Since I have no idea what is in the box, I take it to my room to open without spying eyes.

I hesitate. Because when you don't know anyone who can afford to send you something, receiving an unknown package makes you nervous.

Finally, curiosity pushes me forward. I struggle against the tape holding it closed. I'm sure they have scissors in the office, but I don't want to go there so I continue working until the lid rips open.

On top is a child's toboggan and a pair of mittens—Jonah's size and bright blue with tiny dinosaurs. They take my breath away and I sink onto the bed. Below it is a coat—brand new with the tags still attached and in my favorite color—purple. Tears sting my eyes even as disbelief crowds my thoughts. My hands are shaking. I can't explain the fear that curdles in my insides. When nothing good ever happens for a really long time and then it does, it just doesn't feel right.

Checking again, I confirm it's my name on the box. But who?

I've always believed there are angels watching over Jonah, but they've never sent apparel before.

The coat slides on easily. A comfortable fit and the zipper works all the way to the top. I run my hands over the smooth fabric, noting the absence of snags or tears, then slip my hands into the flannel lined pockets. The fabric feels so soft and warm against my skin that I think I should take it off immediately. I can't get used to something this nice. Maybe one day, but not yet.

A piece of paper brushes against my fingers inside the pocket. I pull it out expecting a note from Inspector Twelve telling me they had proudly inspected this coat and hoped I enjoyed my new outerwear. It makes me laugh. There was a day when I would have thought such a job beneath me. Now who ever Inspector Twelve is seems like an enviably prosperous professional.

It isn't a note from the manufacturer. It's a folded-up scrap of paper torn from a church bulletin. At least, I think it is because the wording says they are celebrating someone's baptism at the late service that day. I unfold it and find a notice on the other side seeking a live-in caregiver for an elderly widow. An address with directions has been handwritten beneath the notice.

My stomach flutters and flips and spins inside me. I read it again then search both sides for a date or even the name of the church. But the paper has been torn so nothing like that remains.

My hopes are higher than they should be. I know this, and yet after last night, I need to feel hopeful again even for just a little while. Going is a risk that might lead to nothing but more rejection. But for Jonah, I'll risk it.

As I leave, I check the clock hanging behind the front desk. Walking is my only form of transportation, and I have to be back in time to meet Jonah when he gets out of school.

It is a long walk and though the day is cold, I unzip my coat as I begin to sweat from the exertion. Or maybe it's the apprehension churning inside me. I tell myself I won't turn back no matter what, and I won't.

The house sits behind a low stone fence in an old but still respectable neighborhood. It is well-kept if not exactly throbbing with life. I stop in front of the house next door, winded from the pace of walking I did to get here. I zip my coat up again even though I'm still damp with sweat. It hides my clothes. Of course, whoever sent the package probably doesn't expect anything better. They know where I live.

What if this is a trick? The thought freezes me in place. Women are abducted and sold into slavery all the time. Has someone set me up? I want to turn and run, but I can't. Something holds me in place. It seems too good to be true. Still, if there's a chance I can do something good for Jonah, I have to know.

Out of habit, I grip the front of my coat even though this one zips to the top. I watch for a movement of the curtains or hidden cameras on the porch, anything that might be a warning. I'm prepared to run at any hint of a threat as I climb the porch steps.

There is no doorbell, so I use my knuckles to knock, softly at first, then again more firmly.

The door opens as if they are waiting for me. I stare into a face that must be the elderly widow from the ad. She looks vaguely familiar, but I can't think of where I might have met her.

"Allie." She whispers my name, as if saying it too loudly might shatter the moment. The love carried in that one softly spoken word roars in my ears. Suddenly we're both crying. I have no idea why. I suspect it's because I haven't heard my name spoken that tenderly in a long time.

"I've waited so long for this moment, please come in." She ushers me into her living room. The smell of freshly baked cookies—snickerdoodles, my favorite—fills the house.

"I don't understand. Do I know you?" I'd really like to sound a little less confused, but this is all I have right now.

"I'm Bonnie Harbor and no, we've never met." She wipes away the tears trying to hide in the deep wrinkles lining her face. "But I most certainly know who you are. And so does she." Bonnie's gaze moves to a spot behind me.

I turn and there she stands. My mother hovers in the doorway leading to the kitchen, tears streaming down her cheeks and leaving dark splotches on the blouse she wears.

Every emotion I imagined having if I ever saw her again was wrong. I only want to go to her, take in her smell, soak in her warmth, get lost in her embrace.

"Mom." The word sounds stiff on my tongue. It's been so long since I've said her name. Five years seems to have aged her more than it should have. She looks pale, frightened maybe, but takes a tentative step toward me. Then we are wrapped in each other's arms, sobbing and laughing and holding on as if one hug could make up for all the years missed.

I pull back. "Where's Dad?"

She looks away, her eyes landing on Bonnie, questioning.

"I'll tell her, Elizabeth." Bonnie places a gentle hand on my mother's shoulder, and my confusion grows. "You get the last of the cookies from the oven. We'll join you in a minute."

I don't like watching my mother leave, even if it is only to the next room. After all this time apart, I feel the urge to cling to her like a child even though I'm a mother now myself.

"We've waited for you all this time. I can't believe you're finally here." Bonnie smiles, but I detect both sadness and joy in the lines around her eyes. "We searched everywhere, but you just vanished. How a pregnant sixteen-year-old can disappear, I don't know. But I do know you certainly have more courage than I did when I was your age. And a lot more grit to raise up that little boy on your own."

"I don't understand what's going on? Is there a job?"

"Perhaps you'll understand better if I show you this first. Come with me." Bonnie heads up the stairs and I follow.

When she stops and motions to a closed door at the far end of the hallway, I open it.

It's a bedroom, made and ready. I recognize my mother's touch in the sunflower bed spread and flowery artwork on the walls. Instinctively, I know it was meant for me.

Then I notice the crib in the corner and turn back to Bonnie.

She laughs. "I guess we won't be needing that anymore, but it was such a sweet looking thing Elizabeth and I just couldn't let it go."

"Was this…" my voice trails. The words sound too ridiculous to speak.

"For you? Yes. We meant for you to come here, but we were too late."

"I don't understand."

"I know you're angry with your father. You have a right to be. But I take the blame for that. My choices helped make him who he is." She clasped her hands in front of her. "I'm your grandmother, your father's mother."

"What about Grandma Lucy?" Am I in a dream or a nightmare?

"Lucy was his adoptive mother. I am his biological mother. When I was sixteen, I too was an unwed pregnant teenager. I put my baby up for adoption. It was the right thing for him—for the both of us. But maybe it wasn't handled as well as it could have been."

Anger flares hot through my veins and I'm ready to bolt. "Is that what this is about? You want me to give Jonah up for adoption?"

She quiets for a moment, then sighs. "Jonah. I didn't know his name. It's a good name."

"I think I need to go now."

"Wait. Please." My mother has been listening. She comes to stand next to Bonnie, blocking the door.

"Why have I never heard Dad was adopted?"

"He forbid us to tell."

"I think he was ashamed, that it made him feel unworthy, like he was a mistake." Bonnie says, tears pooling in her eyes.

"He didn't even know until we were expecting you. The doctors heard something irregular in your heartbeat and wanted to know our family medical history. I think that's the only reason Lucy was finally convinced to tell him. But that's how we found Bonnie."

"But Dad never mentioned her?"

"Something happened to your father when he found out. He'd been lied to all his life, and he couldn't see past his anger. He refused contact with Bonnie. But I stayed in touch. I sent her pictures and artwork you'd drawn." My mother smiles. "Those pictures you colored for the folks at the nursing home? It wasn't a total lie. Bonnie did work there."

"So Dad kicked me out because of what had happened to him? But I don't understand what this is." I spread my arms wide, gesturing at the room where I stand.

"I knew how he would react when he learned you were pregnant. I came straight to Bonnie, and we made a plan. But your father found out and confronted you when I wasn't around. By the time I got home, you were gone. We've looked for you for so long. We never gave up."

I close my eyes, letting the words sink in. "I was so hurt and angry and scared, but I wanted you to come for me. Deep down inside I did. I just didn't want it to be easy. I wanted you to work for it, so I got a fake ID with another name." I look again at my mother. "But why now? How did you know this time?"

"Last night—something made me look out the window. It was so dark and misty, but I knew it was you the moment I saw you. I couldn't let your father know, but I snuck out and followed you."

My mother walks to me and takes my cold hands in her soft, warm ones. It's a touch I would know anywhere. "Allie, will you please forgive me for not protecting you, for not finding you sooner?"

My heart is crumbling, and I realize I was wrong.

Home isn't a building. Home is a heart. And it isn't a place where they have to let you in.

It's a place you never leave.

Questions:

In this conclusion, let's apply the four topics of this book to the story.

The Power of Words

    a. When Bonnie spoke Allie's name, what power did it have?

    b. What effect do you think Bonnie's and Elizabeth's words had on Allie?

    c. What do you think are the most powerful words in the story?

    d. What encouraging words might you need to say to someone to spark hope in their hearts?

The Power of Doing

    a. When Allie's father first learned of her pregnancy, he reacted out of his own pain and sense of shame. What power did his actions have in his family's life?

    b. When Allie was kicked out of her home, she changed her name. What power did that have in her life for the next five years?

    c. When difficult things happen to us, what promises of God can we rely on?

    d. When Allie read the job notice, she was afraid to apply for it because she feared rejection. She took the risk for Jonah's sake. What risks might we need to take on behalf of the God we love and for others?

The Power of Knowing

    a. What "special understanding" of Jonah did his mother have?

    b. What special understanding of us do you think God addresses in Deuteronomy 31:6 and 8?

    c. What comforting promises do these verses give?

    d. How do you think it made Allie feel to know that the one who sent her the package, knew where she lived?

    e. God knows the difficulties and challenges of where we live. What encouragement has He given us regarding that?

    f. Allie didn't know for five years that her mother and Bonnie wanted to make a home for her and her child. How does it affect us to know that God wants to make His home with the one who loves Him (John 14:23)?

The Power of Prayer

    a. Let's speculate a little. What specifics might Bonnie and Elizabeth have been praying for?

    b. Allie once tried to hide from her parents, or make it harder for them to find her. She knew where to find them. What might she have been praying for?

    c. What can we pray for people whose hope is fading?

Contributing Authors
In Alphabetical Order

Karen O. Allen has a passion for music, ministry, and dogs. Recently retired from cancer research, she maintains her position as an organist. Her Bible study *Confronting Cancer with Faith* (www.confrontingcancerwithfaith.com) has brought hope around the world. Connect with Karen on her new Ewe R Blessed Ministries blog (www.ewerblessed.com/blog) that highlights everyday and unexpected blessings.

Lori Altebaumer loves sharing the joys of living a Christ-centered life with others through her writing. With boots on the ground, head in the clouds, and heart in His hands, Lori writes to educate, inspire, encourage, entertain, and spread the love of God. Learn more about Lori at www.lorialtebaumer.com, or on her Facebook page @lorialtebaumerwrites.

Dr. Lori Brown is an educator, consultant, and author who loves inspiring people to find joy and relevance in the Scriptures. She enjoys traveling with her twin sister, volunteering at the local homeless shelter, and writing about effective leadership and safe school practices for various academic publications. She makes her home in Asheville, North Carolina.

Billie Corley, founder of Growing Girls, Gals and Grannies for God, is a writer, speaker, and Bible teacher. She seeks to provide biblical principles which will motivate women to excel in their spiritual walk. Her passion can be summed up in her ministry's slogan "Seeking to Teach, Inspire, and Encourage Women Everywhere for Jesus Christ." Billie resides in Georgia with her husband Ben. You can obtain more information regarding Billie's ministry at www.billiecorley.com.

Jennifer DeFrates is a blogger and speaker who shares the inspirational lessons God teaches in the daily life of a military spouse, adoptive parent, homeschooling mom, and passionate follower of Christ. She writes about the power of seeing God in the mundane bits of her life and how He transforms her daily at *Heaven not Harvard* (http://heavennotharvard.com).

Mary Albers Felkins lives in the North Carolina foothills with her husband Bruce. They have four semi-adult children in their quiver. She can be lured from her writing cave with a party-sized bag of Peanut M&Ms® or an episode of Fixer Upper. In addition to her weekly blog at www.maryfelkins.com, she is an author of contemporary romance. Her first novel, *Call To Love*, is set in Hickory, North Carolina, and it was released in November 2019.

A teacher at heart, Barb Fox loves motivating others to dig deeper into the Word. Research scientist by day and Christian living writer by night, she thanks God for weekends and a husband who keeps life fun even when she sometimes gets a bit too serious.

Karen Fulgham is a freelance writer in biblical concepts for practical Christian living, young women's discipleship, Christian poetry, and other creative writings. Serving community is a lived passion through twenty-nine years of nursing. Karen is a seminary student, while keeping watch as a praying wife, mom, and nana living in Arkansas. Visit glimpsesinwords.wordpress.com, Facebook, or Twitter.

Ron Gallagher is a writer, speaker, teacher, and blogger, as well as a ministry consultant for local churches. His Biblical insights are coupled with down-to-earth humor, satire, and relevant stories, all aimed at promoting *"right side up thinking in an upside down world."* He strives to apply God's truth in a way that stimulates the mind, encourages the heart, and challenges the cultural norm. Check out Ron's blog, www.GallaghersPen.com, and connect with him at www.twitter.com/gallagherspen.

Becky Hitchcock lives and writes in Old Clyattville, a community outside Valdosta, Georgia. She and her high school sweetheart-husband have two grown children. Becky enjoys walking on the beach and collecting vintage Blue Willow china. She is a self-professed technology-phobic, but would love to hear from you at sensitiveonpurpose.blogspot.com.

Mary Holloman is a wife, mother, writer, and Peanut M&Ms® enthusiast. When she's not wrangling her two kiddos, she works and writes for Greensboro Pregnancy Care Center in North Carolina. Mary has written for *Charisma Magazine*, the Christian Broadcasting Network, the Ethics and Religious Liberty Commission, Just 18 Summers, and others. You can read more of her work at maryholloman.com.

Katy Kauffman is an editor of *Refresh Bible Study Magazine*. She is also an award-winning author and a co-founder of Lighthouse Bible Studies. She has taught the Bible to women and teens, and her love for prayer can be seen in her poetry and in the prayers she writes for her Bible studies. Connect with her at www.lighthousebiblestudies.com.

Lisa Kibler is an award-winning writer who lives with her God-sent kitty, Lewis, in Minerva, Ohio. She is a member of the Jerry Jenkins Writers Guild and is a mentor for Word Weavers International. Her unpublished manuscript, *Someplace to be Somebody*, has already won multiple awards. Lisa has contributed to the compilations, *Heart Renovation* and *Feed Your Soul with the Word of God*, and to *Refresh Bible Study Magazine*. Interact with her at www.lisakibler.com.

Jenifer Kitchens seeks to know God and make Him known as a minister's wife, homeschooling mother of three, and writer of Bible studies for all ages. You can follow her blog at DirtyDishwaterHolyHands.wordpress.com.

Barbara Latta's desire is to help others find intimacy with God through a deeper understanding of the power of the Word. She writes a monthly column in her local newspaper and contributes to devotional websites and has stories in several anthologies. She recently published her first book, *God's Maps, Stories of Inspiration and Direction for Motorcycle Riders*, available on Amazon. Barbara's blog can be found at www.barbaralatta.blogspot.com.

Dawn Linton is a Licensed Clinical Social Worker and Chaplain. She provides critical incident response to first responders in the aftermath of trauma, and co-facilitates a faith-based cancer support group at her local church. Dawn lives with her husband Steve in Williamsburg, Virginia.

Dr. Roy E. Lucas, Jr. is an author, retired pastor, and retired Professor of Bible from Clear Creek Baptist Bible College. He lives in the Appalachian Mountains with his wife, Veda. He preaches, teaches, serves as an interim pastor, and leads tours to Israel. His articles appear in LifeWay's *Biblical Illustrator*, *Deacon Magazine*, *Senior Adult Bible Studies for Life*, *Refresh Bible Study Magazine*, and the *Revised Holman Illustrated Bible Dictionary* (2015). Connect with Dr. Lucas at https://truth-travelers.com or drlucas4321@gmail.com.

Jonathan McDuffie is a follower of Christ, husband, father, student pastor, and writer. His passion is helping believers connect with Christ, hear His voice, and experience His transforming power in their lives. Connect with him at jmcdwrites.com.

Marilyn Nutter of Greer, South Carolina, is a contributor to magazines, websites, and compilations. She is a Bible teacher and speaker for women's groups and for grief support. She serves on the women's ministry team at her church. In her life's seasons, she has met God's faithfulness and clings to Lamentations 3:22-23. Visit www.marilynnutter.com to find extraordinary treasures in ordinary and challenging days.

Katherine Pasour is an author, teacher, speaker, and advocate for wellness. She has a passion for service and seeks to nurture others on their journey to achieve and maintain better health. Her Bible studies and blog focus on developing a closer relationship with Jesus and making lifestyle choices for a healthier and happier life in service to our Lord and Savior. Connect with her at www.katherinepasour.com.

Brad Simon is a gifted Bible expositor and Master Storyteller. He's taught Bible studies and served in church leadership for over forty years. Originally from Illinois, Brad and his wife Debbie have made Spartanburg, South Carolina their home for the past twenty-four years. Brad is a retired Master Jeweler and was a popular speaker and author in the jewelry industry. Discover his Bible Teaching Ministry at BWSimon.com.

Jeannie Waters is a retired educator who leads a Bible study for second language learners. She contributed to *Breaking the Chains* and *Heart Renovation: A Construction Guide to Godly Character* (Lighthouse Bible Studies) and two devotional books. Jeannie adores family time and meeting new friends. Visit www.jeanniewaters.com for ideas on Brightening Someone's Day.

Krystal Weeks is a Christian writer who desires to encourage other believers through her words, and who publishes poems and articles to inspire others to spread the living hope of the Gospel. She has a burning desire to minister to the lost and hurting, and a heart for evangelism here at home and abroad. She has participated in mission trips to Mexico, the Dominican Republic, Guatemala, Brazil, and Spain. She gives God the glory for her opportunities to write and to be a witness of His love.

J. D. Wininger is an award-winning writer and speaker who teaches compelling lessons in faith and writes heartfelt devotionals and books to glorify God. He has written for national magazines, CBN.com, and *Refresh Bible Study Magazine*, and he has contributed to several books. When not working his Texas ranch, he and his wife share

God's love in surrounding communities. Follow J. D. at www.twitter.com/JD_Wininger, or at www.jdwininger.com.

As a follower of Jesus Christ and lover of God's Word, Connie Wohlford has been a Bible teacher and ministry leader in her church for many years. She and husband, Guy, live amidst the Blue Ridge Mountains of Virginia. An award-winning author, she writes interactive Bible studies, children's books, and blogs at *God's Word Our Destiny*, http://godswordourdestiny.blogspot.com.

K. A. Wypych is a Christian writer, speaker, and athlete who inspires people to courageously persevere through challenges to reach their dreams and improve their lives. She has published articles and devotionals. Her book, *Ten Iron Principles*, is a Christian living memoir about perseverance and salvation through playing football on a boys' junior varsity team and her road to the Ironman triathlon. Follow her at kawypych.com. Never quit. Defy limits. Courage UP!

Dorcas Asercion Zuniga is a family medicine physician who is also honored to be the wife of her assistant-pastor husband and mother of their teenage son. She is thankful to Yahweh for fulfilling her childhood dream of becoming a writer and grateful for the opportunity to write for *Refresh*, *Broken but Priceless*, *The Magazine*, and other Christian publications.

Group Discussion

These Bible studies were written to be useful for both personal Bible study and group discussion. The stories, illustrations, and examples invite sharing personal insights and comments. The questions at the end of the studies are tailor made to spur personal reflection in quiet times and discussion in group settings.

For an eight-week study, divide the four sections as follows:

Week 1 - The Power of Words, the first five studies
Week 2 - The Power of Words, the next five studies

Week 3 - The Power of Doing, the first five studies
Week 4 - The Power of Doing, the next five studies

Week 5 - The Power of Knowing, the first five studies
Week 6 - The Power of Knowing, the next five studies

Week 7 - The Power of Prayer, the first five studies
Week 8 - The Power of Prayer, the next five studies and Conclusion: "Home"

Once you have discussed the questions from the Bible studies, see whether any of the following questions remain unanswered.

- Which study is the most meaningful to you this week? Why?
- Which illustration or example was the most memorable?
- Is there any particular insight that resonated with you?

May God use these studies to make a joyful difference in your life!

Bibliography

Jones, Alexander, General Editor. *The Jerusalem Bible Reader's Edition*. Garden City, New York: Doubleday & Company, Inc., 1966.

Schofield, J. Chris. *Prayerwalking Made Simple*. Cary, North Carolina: Baptist State Convention of North Carolina, 2018.